MANDATE
THE 7 MOUNTAINS OF GOD

A CANDID LOOK AT CHRISTIANITY'S INFLUENCE ON
THE 7 SPHERES OF CULTURE

Deborah McClendon

Published by Deborah McClendon.
All rights reserved.

©2017 by Deborah McClendon
All rights reserved. No part of this publication may be reproduced, stored electronically, or otherwise transmitted in any form or by any means, including but not limited to electronic, mechanical, photocopying or recording without permission of the author.

Printed in the United States of America

ISBN-13: 978-1981917921
ISBN-10: 1981917926|

Published by Deborah McClendon 2017
Atlanta, GA

Unless otherwise stated, all Scripture citations are from the King James Version, Public Domain.

Cover Design: Jonathan McDougald
Back Cover Photo: Calvin Callendar

DEDICATION

Thank You, Father, for the completion of this book, which I dedicate to You first because You are the Author and Finisher of my faith. Without the guidance of your Holy Spirit, I could not have finished. I thank You for instilling in my heart Your powerful Word and trusting me to use it to discuss the seven spheres of our society that shape our culture. And for that reason alone, I have to dedicate back to You what You have given to me.

I dedicate this book also to my family, friends and my many sisters and brothers in Christ.

TABLE OF CONTENTS

Acknowledgments	vii
Foreword	viii
Introduction	1
The Seven Mountains	
Chapter 1 – Religion	9
Chapter 2 – Media	19
Chapter 3 – Family	25
Chapter 4 – Education	36
Chapter 5 – Arts and Entertainment	43
Chapter 6 – Business	51
Chapter 7 – Government	58
Concluding Thoughts	67
Notes	71

ACKNOWLEDGMENTS

A special thank you to my sister, Doll, for encouraging me, and to Gail and Ms. Thelma for cheering me on and pushing me to the finish line. Shanita and Sandrika—thank you for typing and proofreading. Angela—my deepest appreciation for getting it ready for my editor, Yvonne, for giving it the 'fine tuning' it needed.

Finally, I would like to especially thank Calvin Callendar for the back cover photo.

I appreciate all of you!

FOREWORD

I have known Deborah McClendon for a little over three years. In that short time, I have learned and observed several things about her. First, she has always presented herself as a woman who truly loves God. I am a first-hand witness to her worship, her dedication to Him and His house, and to His children and work. Secondly, while some may say she has a "no nonsense" approach to life, I would have to say it's just Deborah's way of using the Word of God as her guide. Her first response is to show love towards her fellow man. And, it is with love that she writes this book.

When Deborah asked me to write the Foreword, I was a little hesitant. Why? Because I was not sure what I would say. You see, I have read many books on the topic of the Seven Mountains. I have also done plenty of research on social media—which happens to be one of the mountains—and taught classes as well on the subject. So naturally I began to wonder how different would this book be? What new thing could be added to a subject that has been around since the 1970's? How different will this book be from all the others out there? As I began to read Deborah's words, I noticed a significantly huge difference from the other books I have studied on this topic. Deborah's words were written from a heart filled with love for the children of God.

Most books and articles just dispense information and/or statistics. And even fewer ever touch the places in our heart that need strengthening and encouragement. However, Deborah's words are as relevant today as they were 5, 10, 15, even 40 years ago. She writes with clarity and understanding. She writes with a genuine desire to see God's people succeed in life and be all that we can become. With this book, I would have to say, "Mission accomplished"!

As you read the pages, I pray that you are as touched as I was. I pray that you realize that God has a purpose and a plan for your life to effect change in this world for the Kingdom. I pray that you will allow the words in Matthew 9:10. "Thy will be done, in earth as it is in heaven" to become real to you and propel you to your ultimate destiny. You won't regret it.

Apostle John W. Evans, Jr.
Founder and President
God's Army Impacting Nations (GAIN), Inc.
Atlanta, Georgia

INTRODUCTION

THE SETUP: IMPACTING CULTURE

The seven mountains are seven sectors that mold or shape the way we think and view things. Our society is transformed and affected by these sectors in ways that influence the way we all see our own lives and see ourselves through the lives of others. As a matter of consequence, I wrote this book to show how **religion, media, family, education, business, arts and entertainment, and government,** shaped our culture *significantly*.

Additionally I wanted to make a case for how the mindset of every believer in Christ must shift to a Kingdom *mindset (one that exemplifies being a doer of the Word, while improving always in holiness and exemplifying the righteous character that prepares us to rule under Christ as kings and priests. It is a converted, transformed mind that is matured in the Word of God).* This mindset is a prerequisite to bring change to the marketplace, our workplaces and the communities that we share with people every day. After all, Jesus had a marketplace, workplace, and a Kingdom mindset. It didn't matter what circumstances He faced. He remained true to His purpose on earth. He ministered, healed, set at liberty those that were bound…and He enjoyed it!

We must focus on the sacred to be able to break down the walls of the secular by making wise the saints of God in order to bring revival to the workplace. "Wisdom is the principal thing; therefore get wisdom: and with all thy getting, get understanding." (Proverbs 4:7) The Word of God also says, "If it be possible, as much as lieth in you, live peaceably with all men." (Romans 12:18) Know that whatever position you are in at your workplace, you were called by God to be there and it should be seen as your ministry. Our knowledge of the Father has to be developed in such a way that when He speaks to us, we ask no

MANDATE TO INVADE THE 7 MOUNTAINS OF GOD

questions but move on the things that He orders us to do. What we fail to realize is that God's glory will not co-exist with sin, including disobedience.

Our nation and 'mountains', as cited earlier, are full of idol worship, rebellion and wickedness. Our Father has always warned us of such practices. Unfortunately, we haven't always listened, but mocked God instead. Because God loves us so much, He gives us chance after chance. His patience is long. However, He is not to be mocked. Galatians 6:7, 8 state, "Be not deceived; God is not mocked: for whatsoever a man soweth, that shall he also reap. For he that soweth to his flesh shall of the flesh reap corruption; but he that soweth to the Spirit shall of the Spirit reap life everlasting" *(emphasis mine)*. Therefore, we have to recognize the times in which we live. God is raising us up as warriors, His priests, His prophets and prophetesses to take our rightful place in His kingdom, workplace and marketplace. As true believers, we should not let anything separate us from the love of God. For we understand that there is a new order, the one in which He is preparing and equipping us. He's showing us by driving out by deliverance the things that hold and bind us captive. We will be known by the spirit we possess. We will also be known by God's presence in us and upon us. In our places of worship, we have to have kingdom mindsets. In our worshipping, we must not permit the enemy to invade the service with all types of distractions. I have seen a pastor put a member out of his church because after repeated counseling and warning this member continued harassing women in the church. He was literally escorted out of the church. The impact of his removal was very helpful by enabling worship service to continue without distraction and intimidation from the person removed. It also showed that this type of behavior would not be accepted in that church. This is why it is imperative to develop a Kingdom mindset. The true servants of God must come forth. Where are the role models and leaders who will help guide our children to a better life? God is calling for the faithful leaders whose hearts are after His own. He's desiring that we hear and obey His voice and preach the word without fear or selfish ambition.

Every mountain is a ministry. Therefore, every believer who desires to walk in righteousness must prepare themselves for the marketplace and the workplace, which is encompassed by one of the seven mountains. So when we are trained by the Spirit that works in us, we can go into the marketplace and workplace and show the love of God and win souls for the coming day of Christ. In either place, we must decide to accept the call that God has placed on us to do His will. We must be awakened to our new identities that he has predestined for us because there is so much work to be done. We must take our talents and spiritual gifting and bring change to a dying nation, regardless of which 'mountain' we serve in. Like never before, it is time to really get to know "our Father which art in heaven." Getting to know others and ourselves is essential, but we need to spend time with our Father so that we can REALLY know Him. Each of us are assigned to various jobs in the marketplace and workplace to do the will of God and to bring light into all the dark places that are plagued with injustice and greed. When watching what's going on in today's news, it seems to me that Biblical morality is on the decline and has been replaced by hatred, prejudices and so many things that keep us divided as people and as a nation. A house divided against itself will not stand.

It's time to be about our Father's business. Say "**Yes**" to the call, then do the work. We will accept our various assignments knowing that there are no "little you's and big I's." As believers, we have become one by the blood of Jesus. God has created each of us with unique abilities, strengths, desires and interests to choose a profession and various occupations that will help us fulfill our God-given destinies in the marketplace and the workplace. But we still have to become full-time men and women of faith in God with the faith of God. From what I can infer from the definition of the Hebrew word "avodah", a scriptural

MANDATE TO INVADE THE 7 MOUNTAINS OF GOD

word meaning both "work" and "worship", I believe God sees our work as worship. In the past, some of us concluded that a full-time Christian in ministry was more holy and committed than one serving in the secular environment. But now we must realize that each area of the marketplace is just as important as another.

The Body of Christ has to infiltrate each of these mountains with a Kingdom mindset. We will then become more effective in reaching souls, seizing territories and possessing the gates of the enemy. God has called us to be excellent in everything that we do. Because of Him, we have access to the more excellent way of doing His great works. I John 4:4 lets us know that "Greater is he that is in us than he that is in the world." When we are filled with God's Spirit, He reveals to us His secrets. By being filled with God's Spirit in this way, men, women and children will take their rightful places in the Kingdom, doing the will of the Father with signs and wonders following.

These times are critical. Isaiah 2:2-3 states: "And it shall come to pass in the last days that the mountain of the Lord's house shall be established in the top of the mountains and shall be exalted above the hills; and all nations shall flow unto it. And many people shall go and say, Come ye, and let us go up to the mountain of the Lord, to the house of the God of Jacob; and he will teach us of his ways, and we will walk in his paths: for out of Zion shall go forth the law, and the word of the Lord from Jerusalem." We have to be fully clothed in God's glory to be activated in oneness of heart. Regardless of where you are in your walk with Christ, do not cease praying. Stay the course God will help you.

FULFILLING YOUR MOUNTAIN ASSIGNMENT – TO THE END

These mountains will be the foundation of governments, society and culture during the millennial reign of Jesus. When ungodly spirits or persons occupy these relevant spheres **(family, religion, government,**

business, media, arts and entertainment and education), then they control the harvest (e.g., souls, information, global finance). If the enemy controls these mountains, he will kill, steal and destroy everything in his path, dismantling the very thing that God has placed in our hands—the very thing which is part of the covenant he made at the beginning of time. This covenant empowers us to inherit covenant blessings, to bring change, peace and the love of God to every mountain that affects lives. If the enemy gains control of a mountain, then he can also gain control of the minds of people in that mountain, and lead them into lawlessness, greed, dishonor, oppression, depression and all forms of debauchery.

Saints of the Most High God, we must awaken and rise to the occasion and influence what happens on these mountains. Here's how we can do this:

"Ye are the salt of the earth: but if the salt has lost his savor, wherewith shall it be salted? It is thenceforth good for nothing, but to be cast out, and to be trodden under foot of men. Ye are the light of the world. A city that is set on an hill cannot be hid. Neither do men light a candle and put it under a bushel, but on a candlestick; and it giveth light unto all that are in the house. Let your light so shine before men, that they may see your good works, and glorify your Father which is in heaven" Matthew 5:13-16.

Jesus used the concepts of salt and light to depict our role as His followers and positive influencers. Salt in the Middle East was used to preserve food because of a lack of refrigeration. As believers in Christ, we act as preservers to the world in that we preserve it from the sin that plagues our societies. Salt is also used as a flavor enhancer and seasoning. Similarly, as believers in Christ, we make life better.

MANDATE TO INVADE THE 7 MOUNTAINS OF GOD

We must also be light to those around us by bringing God's Word, His Spirit, His light and His life to the darkness that prevails around us. Before we can work in the Kingdom of our mountain of influence, we must have a heart for God's will to be done. For starters, we have to be in a covenant relationship with Him, being fully committed. Furthermore, we have to know His voice and how to listen for instructions. We have to understand God's authority as well as respect it. Obedience is the principle thing with that. It is truly necessary to meet God's authority and possess a basic knowledge of what it is. By the way, God's words are His authority. Isaiah 55:11 states, " So shall my word be that goeth forth out of my mouth: it shall not return unto me void, but it shall accomplish that which I please, and it shall prosper in the thing whereto I sent it." And, we must understand the power of God's words as stipulated in Hebrews 4:12. "For the word of God is quick, and powerful, and sharper than any two-edged sword, piercing even to the dividing asunder of soul and spirit, and of the joints and marrow, and is a discerner of the thoughts and intents of the heart." Even when Saul set out with an assignment to destroy the church, God was not worried because He knew that His plan by far outweighed the plan of Saul. After Saul's conversion experience on that Damascus road, and the subsequent name change (the Apostle Paul!), he learned to respect the authority of God and to obey God at all costs. Subsequently, Saul impacted nations, his culture at the time, and eventually the world!

Our influence in the mountain God has assigned us cannot be established through manipulation or fear. Rather, we must daily bring the love of Christ, His salvation plan and the authority of His Word to the workplace and marketplace.

When we come to know that we are commissioned by God to do His will, acceptance of that call is inevitable. We must not be like Saul once was and "kick against the pricks," (Acts 9:4-6), since it will only delay the spiritual assignment given to us by God. If you are surely chosen, kicking the prick only brings more pain and suffering. Just say "yes". Jesus has sent out His wonderful saints to do the works of the Kingdom. As the Body of Christ, we can then work together, regardless of our occupation, teaching and showing others about the Kingdom of God with boldness, power, love and compassion, using the keys of the Kingdom which are His power, authority and anointing, to bind demonic influences and to loose people from satanic bondage.

Knowing the will of God also enables us to help others to discover the power that is within them as well. Each of us must know who we are in Christ and the tremendous power we possess as Disciples of Christ. The Word of God puts it this way: "Greater is He that is in you than he that is in the world" (I John 4:4). Being the consistent adversary, be prepared to put up a fight with the enemy. To do this, start with being armed with wisdom, knowledge and understanding. You will also need to keep yourself covered daily in the armor of God. Here's how Ephesians 6:10-18 puts it.

> "Finally, my brethren, be strong in the Lord, and in the power of his might. Put on the whole armour of God that ye may be able to stand against the wiles of the devil. For we wrestle not against flesh and blood, but against principalities, against powers, against the rulers of the darkness of this world, against spiritual wickedness in high places. Wherefore take unto you the whole armour of God that ye may be able to withstand in the evil day, and having done all, to stand. Stand therefore, having your loins girt about with the truth, and having on the breastplate of righteousness; and your feet shod with the preparation of the gospel of peace; Above all, taking the shield of faith, wherewith ye shall be able to quench all the fiery darts of the wicked. And take the helmet of salvation, and the sword of the Spirit, which is the word of God: Praying always with all prayer and supplication in the Spirit, and

MANDATE TO INVADE THE 7 MOUNTAINS OF GOD

watching thereunto with all perseverance and supplication for all saints."

Because our God hears us and is with us, it doesn't matter into which mountain our careers and callings may lead us. The Word of God is a lamp to our feet; it lights our path (Psalm 119:105). The Word and the Spirit of God always let us see what is ahead of us. Even if you fall in influencing your mountain, get up and try again for though the righteous fall seven times, they rise again. In Job 5:19, God promises, "He shall deliver thee in six troubles: yea, in seven there shall no evil touch thee."

Remember your mountain assignment and pursue it!

CHAPTER ONE

THE RELIGION MOUNTAIN

"But seek ye first the kingdom of God, and His righteousness; and all these things shall be added unto you" (Matthew 6:33).

WHAT IS THE RELIGION MOUNTAIN OF GOD?

I believe that in the Religion Mountain, real change takes place. Once we are born again by God's Spirit, we are adopted into God's family of believers who are converted, transformed and matured in the knowledge of God. We must take His yoke upon ourselves to learn of Him, for His yoke is easy and the burden is light. Now, more than ever, our pastors and leaders are accountable and subject to the teaching of the flock to "learn of Him", "mature in the knowledge of God", and be transformed. Most recognize the importance of the small window of time they have to prepare their flocks for battle in the world and set about the business of doing so. At the same time, not all pastors and ministers have equipped their people to truly impact culture in the workplace or marketplace. Each believer has an assignment and each of us has special abilities and strengths with which to perform the work of the Kingdom of God, whether the setting is the workplace or marketplace.

WHAT TO DO TO BE INFLUENTIAL ON THE RELIGION MOUNTAIN

To have influence in the Mountain of Religion, we must first be born again and we must diligently seek Him, for He rewards those that do so. We have to find a place where we can worship Him and where the teaching is strong on obeying God's Word. Sensitivity to the voice of His Spirit and His Word is crucial in our walk with Him. Through them, He shares His secrets and reveals strategic plans of operation in the

MANDATE TO INVADE THE 7 MOUNTAINS OF GOD

Kingdom that need to be accomplished. There are key things we must do: First, II Timothy 2:15, 16 and 19 state to

> *Study to show thyself approved unto God, a workman that needeth not to be ashamed, rightly dividing the word of truth. But shun profane and vain babblings: for they will increase unto more ungodliness...Nevertheless the foundation of God standeth sure, having this seal, the Lord knoweth them that are His. Let everyone that nameth the name of Christ depart from iniquity.*

To God be the glory, All of our iniquities (lawlessness, disobedience, sin) are overcome by His power.

Secondly, get wisdom, get knowledge and get understanding.

Thirdly, we must worship the King. Worship is the protocol for entering into His presence. Worship is the highest level of praise. In worship, our lives and physical bodies become the praise offered to Him. Worship transports you into the Holy of Holies which is the inner chamber and the sacred dwelling place of the King of Glory for the exchange of love, adoration, service, and fulfillment. Ultimately, the purpose of our worship is to focus on Him and His many beautiful attributes. Precept upon precept, we learn, we grow and we seek to understand His power working within us. We have to understand the power of the God we serve. There are heights and depths to obtaining more and more of the Father. As we draw near to Him, He will draw near to us. His love will be shed abroad in our hearts.

With our salvation comes possession of the power of God, along with the Holy Spirit who is our Comforter, the Spirit that will never leave us nor forsake us. We need pure hearts and clean hands. Consider the following verses in II Timothy.

> *Who concerning the truth have erred, saying that the resurrection is past already; and overthrow the faith of some. Nevertheless the foundation of God standeth sure, having this seal. The Lord knoweth those that are his and let everyone that nameth the name of Christ depart from iniquity. But in a great house there are not only vessels of gold and of silver, but also of wood and of earth; and some to honour, and some to dishonour. If a man therefore purge himself from these, he shall be a vessel unto honour, sanctified, and meet for the master's use, and prepared unto every good work.* II Timothy 2:18-21.

In order to be effective in the Religion Mountain, the power of God will have to be demonstrated through us in order to show others the true manifestation of His ability. When we allow His Spirit to rule in our hearts, we learn so much about Our Father, for He speaks to us through our hearts. Let Him in and let Him take charge. Whatever we believe in our hearts will be so. David was a man after God's own heart. Psalms 19:14 states, "Let the words of my mouth, and the meditation of my heart, be acceptable in thy sight, O LORD, my strength, and my redeemer." The condition of our hearts determines whether or not the Word of God will take root and spring into a life overflowing with the love and power of God that will effectively shine light into the dark places of the Mountains that dictate culture.

It is imperative to understand that as the Body of Christ, we are all on the same team. We all have assigned abilities and gifts. Some gifts may be similar, but differences come out in the way they manifest themselves in different people. God is creative and always finds ways to show people who he is. We all learn on different levels in various ways. But when we understand the concept of God's Word, our job simply stated is this: believe and trust God. There are apostles, prophets, pastors, preachers and teachers, and still others who are called to work miracles and show gifts of healing. There are yet more who are called

MANDATE TO INVADE THE 7 MOUNTAINS OF GOD

to the helps ministries, and then there are governmental gifts. In all these giftings, we must remember that to whom much is given, much is required. I Corinthians 12:31 commands us, "But covet earnestly the best gifts..." Our Father will order our steps and show us a better way for He has plans to prosper us and not harm us, to give us hope and a future (Jeremiah 29:11). All we need to do is trust and believe, have faith in Him, and to be doers of the Word and not hearers only. We must love each other unconditionally for our Father is no respecter of persons and neither should we be. We are grafted together through our Father; there is one faith and one baptism and one Lord who is Jesus the Christ. We are His family and a threefold cord is not easily broken. There is a standard to which the children of God are held. We must hold each other accountable, helping one another to succeed in every good way. If we are seeking a life of immortality, we cannot live an unholy life. Every weight, such as unforgiveness, bitterness, doubt, fear, and unbelief, just to name a few, must be laid aside.

In our walk with our Savior, it is impossible to please Him without faith. When we operate out of just head knowledge, we are operating out of a carnal mindset (leaning to our own understanding) and it soon leads to destruction, pride, selfishness, greed and arrogant spirits. But when we operate out of our heart knowledge of our Lord and Savior Jesus Christ and our head knowledge, we are successful in everything we encounter because we then have wisdom, knowledge and understanding and our guidance comes from the Holy Spirit, for He lives in our hearts.

The Body of Christ is connected by the same Spirit as stated in Romans 8:14-17.

> *For as many as are led by the spirit they are the sons of God. For ye have not received the spirit of bondage again to fear: but ye have received the Spirit of adoption, whereby we cry, Abba,*

Father. The Spirit itself beareth witness with our spirit, that we are the children of God: And if children, then heirs; heirs of God, and joint-heirs with Christ; if so be that we suffer with him, that we may be also glorified together.

We must worship Him in spirit and in truth. True worshippers of God are on the rise all over the world. They are preparing for spiritual battle. We are preparing to do greater works than Christ Jesus, because He went back to his Father and there He makes intercession for us daily.

Every day presents an opportunity to give your life wholly to Christ. This opportunity is a chance for salvation which prepares for you a place in eternity. Eternity is the epitome of ***immortality*** – a life forever with our Lord and Savior Jesus Christ. Allow Him to do the work in you that needs to be done by making over your heart with Kingdom order and principles that please Him and assures you a life of immortality in His presence. God alone will lead us to truth and to righteousness. He will order our steps. We can take steps, but only He can direct a clear path for our lives. By renewing the right spirit within us, He enables us to have a tender heart of flesh that is sensitive to the voice of God. The issues of our behavior are not about whether we make a mistake, but rather whether or not we obey God. Ezekiel 11:19-21 says,

And I will give them one heart, and I will put a new spirit within you; and I will take the stony heart out of their flesh, and will give them an heart of flesh: That they may walk in my statutes, and keep mine ordinances, and do them: and they shall be my people, and I will be their God. But as for them whose heart walketh after the heart of their detestable things and their abominations, I will recompense their way upon their own heads, saith the Lord GOD.

As our Father continually prepares us for the tasks ahead, I pray for

MANDATE TO INVADE THE 7 MOUNTAINS OF GOD

the faith and confidence that we will need as a universal church body. I pray for oneness and singleness of heart and trusting that God will perfect all that concerns us. While we understand that we will have trials and tribulations, Psalm 34:19 encourages us. "Many are the afflictions of the righteous: but the Lord delivereth him out of them all."

I pray that we will have patience and compassion in all manner of business related to the Mountain of Religion. We must believe that if God is for us, nothing and no one can ultimately prevail against us. And as for all of the assignments of the enemy, since God did not send them, I pray that He will cancel them. For God is Jehovah Nissi, the Lord our banner. Isaiah 54:15-17 assures us this.

> *Behold they shall surely gather together, but not by me: whosoever shall gather together against thee shall fall for thy sake. Behold I have created the smith that bloweth the coals in the fire, that bringeth forth an instrument for his work; and I have created the waster to destroy. No weapon formed against thee shall prosper; and every tongue that shall rise against thee in judgement thou shalt condemn. This is the heritage of the servants of the Lord, and their righteousness is of me, saith the Lord.*

Through the power of this promise, we can bind together and secure the borders of the Religion Mountain.

This is not the time to be spiritually sleepy. Arise, awake and let' us do the work of our Father, Jesus the Christ. This warfare between the enemy and our Father has been fought for centuries. The good news is this: the weapons of our warfare are not carnal but spiritual to the pulling down of all strongholds (II Corinthians 10:4). We possess the territories of the enemy through warfare training and God's possession of power. God desires that His Church have the control, authority and influence over the powers of darkness in this mountain. It is imperative that the Body of Christ knows both when it has stepped into enemy territory and when the enemy enters our territory.

As we step into higher authority in the Mountain of Religion, we realize that there are different levels: the top, the middle and the base. The top has very strong leaders that map out strategies of warfare for the Kingdom. They are converted, sold-out believers in Christ that take no thought for the job at hand. They press the enemy out to the middle of the mountain.

The middle of the mountain consists of God's people that force the enemy out through additional prayer and fasting. At this level of the mountain, the fight is just as aggressive as it is at the top, but more pressure is applied to pull down and press out the enemy to the bottom of the mountain.

At the bottom of the mountain, more believers await to break every chain, causing a more defeated state, having destroyed all the works of the enemy and cancelling his assignments. When we fight the good fight for the Kingdom, we have a life of immortality promised to us.

When God calls upon us and we answer "yes" to the call, we are already equipped. The manifestation comes after each life lesson. The Word of God says He teaches our hands to war. "Blessed *be* the Lord my strength, which teacheth my hands to war, *and* my fingers to fight" (Psalm 144:1). The more we learn about our faith and the power that is in His Name, we will hear from heaven and see Him perform His word and His Word, which will never return to Him void. Our faith increases when we put the Word of God into action. For instance, the Word of God says that if we resist the devil, he will flee from us (James 4:7). But if we never try the Word, how can we know that it works or not? When we become doers of God's Word and not merely hearers, not only does our faith increase, but also our relationship with our Father becomes

MANDATE TO INVADE THE 7 MOUNTAINS OF GOD

more intimate. And as the Body of Christ, we must have faith that the Word works in order to effective in the Mountain of Religion.

We must also perform duties within our places of worship. Administrators, ushers, intercessory prayer warriors, prophets with signs following, deliverance teams, maintenance crews, musicians, choirs, youth ministers and countless others, are all necessary to taking this mountain. Impacting the Mountain of Religion requires all of these giftings and talents. All are important to God.

To be successful at taking this mountain, we must understand that we are in covenant with God and each other. We truly have to try to honor those things that bring peace to our lives and honor God at the same time. If your call is leadership, then serve with respect, love and compassion. If it is intercession, be diligent in prayer. If it is praise and worship, doesn't our Father deserve the type of atmosphere where He can dwell amongst His people? Whatever it is, let us do it to the glory of God. Willingly share your gifts with the Body of Christ. This should be our most reasonable service and desire. Once we totally commit to being the salt and light of the earth, we will totally experience a true fellowship with God. We are on assignment to show forth God's love and to allow His Grace to be amongst us when we gather with others – cheerfully sharing the Good News of God. As we rise to our destined life with God and each other, it is imperative that our children are taught of our Father as well. We are responsible for reinstating "the village." The village includes sisters and brothers in Christ who are willing to take some time to instill in all of our children values such as respect for self and for others. Kingdom-minded parents recognize that they must parent other people's children as well as their own. For instance, if a baby's shoe needs tying, tie his shoe and take some time to teach him or her how to do it. We must love our neighbors as ourselves. There is nothing wrong with telling a young man that it is okay to wear a belt, and not to disrespect himself by wearing his pants half-way down his legs. We are a royal priesthood and a chosen generation. Everywhere we go, and everything we do should reflect our relationship with God our Father. Again, we are always on assignment, and we need each other.

As I have been walking this path of working out my salvation with fear and trembling (Philippians 2:12), I have come to the conclusion that there is always so much more to know and understand about God. For example, He desires to show us and to teach us His statutes as we take His yoke upon us and learn of Him. He has said that His yoke is easy and His burden is light (Matthew 11:30). As for me, I desire to establish a more intimate relationship with Him by really getting to know him as my Father. I am so glad that our Father forgives our sin and gives us second chances. We can begin again with a fresh, clean slate. Surely, dying to the flesh is a daily process that takes time, but I'm willing to take the time necessary to make me a better person, prepared for the work to have influence in the Mountain of Religion. What about you? I have decided that I want to know all that a daughter can know about her Father. I have faith and believe that our God has the most excellent way of doing everything. I seek Him because I can trust Him to order my steps. He says He will perfect all that concerns us. He also creates in us a clean heart and renews the right spirit within us. Holy Spirit will bring to our remembrance all that He teaches us.

Taking this mountain requires a whole lot of trust, patience, and the love of the Father. On this path, we will hit some low valleys, some muddy ditches, brooks will dry up, and people will come and go from your life. Brokenness surely comes for whatever reason. Some of these lows may result from self-inflicted iniquities but others are just life. When we give God total preeminence over our lives, He uses the circumstances to shape and mold us into the people He needs us to become for the effectual work in His Kingdom. The good news is that God is preparing us for what is ahead. God alone has the plan. He

MANDATE TO INVADE THE 7 MOUNTAINS OF GOD

transforms, converts, and matures us in such a way that we know it is Him working in our life on behalf of the Gospel of Christ. He promised never to leave us nor forsake us.

Furthermore, we have to have faith and take seriously the task of salvation that is set before us. Most of the time, the stance that Job had seems to be the one to take. That is, we must have a faith that is unshakable, trusting in God to do over and abundantly above all that we can ask or think, and to provide for us all that we need, which are the Holy Spirit, wisdom, knowledge, and understanding. I see Job as a righteous man of God, full of faith. Out of all the things that happened to Job, he did not waiver in his faith. Instead, he demonstrated a patience almost incomprehensible to human nature. However, to have faith in God to that extent is very possible and very probable if we would only believe. Job did not allow iniquity to abound in his life. This is one thing that becomes a focal point to the born-again Christian, to rid our lives of sin. So when you and I said "yes" to God, that alone was an act of faith acknowledging we wanted His rule in our lives. I want Him to teach me His statutes and to help me to be a doer of His Word and to give honor unto Him in all that I do. My relationship with my Father is an intimate connection that is fueled on love and forgiveness. As I die to the old man, my walk becomes one of love and forgiveness to all of mankind.

So you and I must allow God to press out of us all the things that are not pleasing to Him, being mindful of how we treat others. Our identity as Abba's (Daddy's) children should shape our existence and relationship to Him. The iniquities and complexities of life that we deal with daily allow no energy to be judgmental, no energy to hate others or lack mercy, discriminate, or to accuse the poor. We must love everyone and hate no one. As we walk together in oneness, let us hold each other accountable in a loving way that pleases God and keeps peace among us.

CHAPTER TWO

THE MEDIA MOUNTAIN

News Outlets | Radio | Internet | Journalism | Marketing
Public Speaking | Technology

WHAT IS THE MOUNTAIN OF MEDIA?

This particular sphere of societal influence is replete with various modes of communication that are virtually worldwide and powerful enough to change lives and people's perspective at almost the drop of a hat. I am talking, of course, about media which include some of the following: television, news outlets, newspapers, computers, technology (e.g., graphics, video, images, etc.), marketing, public speaking, radio, and the internet to name a few. As you may know these media are a means of communication that reaches large numbers of people every single day, around the clock. That so many media fall into this realm of God's mountain, the term multimedia—a collection of different types of media or the ability to handle information correctly—would not be out of place and is probably more accurate and inclusive of all that is a part of this mountain. Because of the power of this mountain, believers called to it have to take a stand on the Word of God and be cognizant of their character and reputation, both of which can be easily compromised under the influence of some entities that control various media. At all times, believers in this sphere must show the love of God when, say, reporting the news about incidents involving any people group. Love and character matter to God. Read how Paul put it in I Thessalonians 5:21-23.

Prove all things; hold fast to that which is good. Abstain from all appearances of evil. And the very God of peace sanctify you wholly; and I pray God your whole spirit and soul and body be preserved blameless unto the coming of our Lord Jesus Christ.

MANDATE TO INVADE THE 7 MOUNTAINS OF GOD

HOW THE BELIEVER CAN IMPACT THE MEDIA MOUNTAIN

Believers in this sphere of influence must gather facts, seek truth, and stay under the guidance and influence of the Holy Spirit and maintain faith in Jesus Christ. You should desire to abound in Christian grace so that you will of the Spirit reap a life of immortality. You should also avoid compromise, persevere to receive the fulfillment of God's precious promises.

Because iniquities (sins) are sometimes committed unknowingly, I suggest believers wishing to operate in this mountain and be influential take inventory of their motives often. In short, introspection is necessary. Look how David puts it in Psalm 139:23. "Search me, O God, and know my heart: try me, and know my thoughts." When working this mountain, our hearts need to be pure so that the news being reported is not compromised by conforming to the ways of the world. We should be mindful to do good, especially in the business of reporting and disseminating news and information.

A godly reporter, writer, blogger, etc., should trust in the Lord more than him/herself and be a wise man or woman in the Word. When we have a Kingdom mindset, we become one with God and the anointing that He has entrusted to us. God's Word is powerful and sharper than any two-edged sword. Remember that you have been made the light of the world and that light produces truth. Sometimes by just discerning we understand principles and how they work.

In the Media Mountain, you have to seek truth and be a doer of the Word of truth. As you honor God by honoring truth – the whole truth – he places in you the ability to find success in all ways. He favors those that seek truth, honor truth, love truth and those whose souls are full of the truth. People expect to trust the truth that is reported. You must not be afraid of telling the truth. Life is a learning process and how we perceive it is how we will live it. Our Father is holding your hand, and nothing happens to you unless He permits it. Our enemy's power is limited. The problem is that there are some voices in Media that cause us to have doubt and unbelief. But Father God has already given us the victory. We are the head not the tail; we are more than conquerors in Christ Jesus. The angels of the Lord go before us and make 'crooked places straight' (Isaiah 40:4). We can speak and move mountains! The enemy may come in like a flood, but he will have to flee!

In order to see God's transforming power manifested to bring change in any workplace, we have to accept the ministerial call on our life. We have to commit to the development and salvation of others in the workplace. Every believer is expected to live a holy life and lifestyle, not subjecting ourselves to the things that displease our Father. As stated before, there may be a specific sphere or mountain of culture or combination of several of these mountains to which you may be called and equipped to handle. Seeking God for divine revelation and guidance is a must in order to flourish and to be faithful where He places you.

Do all that you do with excellence. The reward is far greater than any risk that you take for the sake of the Kingdom. There may be times that people you work with or for will give you a hard time. Stay focused, grounded and speak grace until they become your footstool. Keep our Father as your focus and as the purpose in all of your work environment. It does not matter how badly bosses and co-workers may treat you. Love them anyway, for you are anointed for this work. You are anointed to do the work our Father has called you to do. Seek God and seek to maintain a Kingdom mindset. Spend time in the Word daily. When we do our own ministerial work for Him in the Kingdom, we worship Him and honor him by being obedient to the task which we are called to do. It is important to our Father, so make it a priority to work for the Lord. Psalm 90:17 says, "And let the beauty of the LORD our God be upon us: and establish thou the work of our hands upon us; yea, the work of our hands establish thou it." And Proverbs 22:29

MANDATE TO INVADE THE 7 MOUNTAINS OF GOD

promises, "Seest thou a man diligent in his business? he shall stand before kings; he shall not stand before mean men."

Unfortunately, oftentimes in our society, some have become accustomed to being the highlight of the news in a negative way. After the storyline has been given, if the reporter does not give the race or gender of the person who committed a crime, and at times it may be automatically assumed that the individual is a minority. Major news outlets often display minorities and other cultures in a very negative way. But Acts 10:34 plainly states, "Then Peter opened his mouth and said, God is no respecter of persons." God's love has been given to all of us and He has not changed His mind about sharing His love with anyone. When reporting is unfair or inaccurate, this actually points to the influence of the adversary and the kingdom of darkness.

Sadly, propaganda seems to be the driving force behind what is reported in the media today. This only further divides people in our society. Propaganda can be loosely defined as misleading information meant to cause a person or persons to adopt a particular point of view. Even though this information is carefully selected and may be true or false (usually the latter), it is used to impose potentially harmful ideas on others. As a believer in the Media Mountain, you are responsible for gathering accurate information. At best, we the viewers and readers, deserve to know the truth whether it is good or bad. Your covenant with God to not compromise and to do His will is a big deal. When we are out of alignment with the truth of God's Word, as a culture we more easily fall into the snare of the enemy.

Taking a stand against the things that you know are wrong can help spark change and effect transformation for the benefit of your assigned community, state, region, or even the nation. Taking a stand for right should become a top priority for you. God is with you. Just as there is a code of ethical conduct and requirements where you work, so are there ordinances and commands in Christ Jesus for the workplace He has placed you. Therefore, truthfully report all news regardless of the race, gender, color or creed of the people involved. There is not a race of people that does not have unbecoming behaviors. Romans 3:23, 24 says to all of us, "For all have sinned, and come short of the glory of God; being justified freely by his grace through the redemption that is in Christ Jesus." His grace is sufficient for all of us.

In this field of work, it would be particularly damaging to possess such traits as arrogance, a drive for power that compromises your integrity, selfish ambition, bigotry, insensitivity, or anything else that could affect your ability to communicate news accurately and objectively, and that would subsequently cause an even greater divide among the citizenry of this great country. If God called you to the Mountain of Media, then you are to shine the love of God in the dark places of it. Where there is unfair reporting, lost integrity, injustices, racial or cultural biases, and the compromising of the truth, you must bring God's light and order. He would have you to restore fairness, balance, integrity and truth, and to respect the different groups of people affected by the news being reported. For instance, there are times it feels that leaders are under attack from the media when all that seems to be reported is scandalous and detrimental. But ALL people groups deserve fairness in reporting. There is so much at stake as to how we the viewers perceive the news being reported. If news is negatively reported, then the impact is that it will be negatively received. It is your duty as a Kingdom reporter to report news from a morally correct standpoint that will resonate with the viewers. All we want is unbiased truth. Although the pressure to taint the news in one direction or another may be great, with God leading and guiding you, you can overcome the temptation, do the right thing and receive God's protection and blessing on your life and career the whole while. What a blessing this is. Simply allow your steps to be guided and ordered by the Lord. Demand the respect you deserve by not compromising and conforming to unfairness in the mainstream media.

MANDATE TO INVADE THE 7 MOUNTAINS OF GOD

Lastly, reporting incidents not only involve having others respect you, but it also means you should respect your viewership by being upfront and transparent. For example, we need to know the truth about the killings of unarmed people or the people who die for no reason in the custody of our police. What's really going on behind the scenes that media outlets don't want us to know? Where are the truth monitors that engage these stories on a daily basis? Be that person – stand up and say that this is wrong. Be the person who viewers look forward to seeing on a daily basis because your reporting style is based on truth, and the compassion or mercy of God is reflected in everything that you report. Be consistent. Ask God for the wisdom, knowledge and understanding that you will need to have influence in this sphere. Lean not to the way you believe things should be; rather acknowledge God and He will give you direction at every turn. If this is your career choice then you are appointed, equipped, and destined for greatness to restore this mountain to the godly mountain it was intended to be.

Stay strong and be courageous as you take this Media Mountain...in Jesus' Name.

CHAPTER THREE

THE FAMILY MOUNTAIN

Marriage Enrichment | Parenting Forums | Motherhood Role
Fatherhood Role | Counseling | Traditional Family Values
Family Altars

WHAT IS THE FAMILY MOUNTAIN?

The center of the covenant activity of God is the family. Scripturally, covenants are promises, pledges or arrangements, chiefly between God and man, but also between spouses, friends, families or even nations. They often differ from simple contractual agreements in that they are binding for life and can even be enforced generationally, lasting long after the persons making the original agreement pass on.

Fathers, mothers, children and the extended relatives all play a part in the Scriptural idea of covenant. The Old Testament's teaching about family is embodied in the first chapters of the Torah, which comprises the five books of Moses. The word Torah is derived from the Hebrew verb "garah" which means "to throw, to shoot (as an arrow) or to win at." It pertains to guidance, instruction, commandments and law. However, the Torah should not be considered simply in a legal sense, but also, a lifestyle illustrated by the relationship between God and Israel.

One of the covenant commandments found in Genesis, the first Book of the Torah, is to have children that God may bless them. "And God blessed them, and God said to them, be fruitful, and multiply, and replenish the earth and subdue it (*bring under control, overcome, conquer*): and have dominion over the fish of the sea, and over the fowl of the air, and over every living thing that moveth upon the earth"

MANDATE TO INVADE THE 7 MOUNTAINS OF GOD

(Genesis 1:28). With this, we have a sense of wisdom, knowledge and understanding of the family union. It is believed that marriage between one man and one woman is the biblical foundation for family. Unfortunately, in American culture today, God's original plan for the family structure has been sacrificed and therefore is broken on many levels.

The conditions of life that have generated the family forum – the focal points of family life – may have changed; however, the key element that has remained the same through the years, is the need of children to be raised by two parents – a mother and a father. Please note, even though our society has been modernized and has become more complex, I believe children need Godly parents who can provide an enormous amount of love, training and emotional security in order for them to succeed in life.

On this mountain, marriage is the relationship God established to produce and raise children. For this reason, married couples should remain in covenant with each other, particularly when they have children. Husbands and wives must commit to keeping the marriage vows they made to one another for a lifetime. Today, vows and marriages are declining due to willful sins and broken covenants. Couples must resist temptations such as adultery and divorce so that the family life will be what God intended it to be.

In the event the marriage looks to end in divorce, I strongly suggest the couple seek counseling and do all that can be done to avoid termination.

I am a divorcee. I know firsthand the emotions and stress it causes. Not only for the husband and wife, but also the whole family. When you do all that you can do to make it work, sometimes it's just not enough. We stop communicating, we stop loving each other and the union falls apart. I know now that Jesus is the vine we are the branches, and if we abide in Him and He in us, we will bear much fruit. Apart from Him, we can do nothing. Sometimes the branches of marriage wither and fall off, taking with it love, compassion, patience, longsuffering, and respect for one another. However, if we stay connected to the vine, there is much life still in the vine to help build again what was broken. That vine is Jesus our Lord who can help couples honor the marriage covenant and be the great families he intended us all to be.

God commands husbands to love their wives in the same way that Christ loves the Church. Some husbands have loved everyone except their own wives. Some wives have also played a part in the failure of the marriage covenant. Note this admonishment on marital relationships in Ephesians 5:21-28.

> [21]*Submitting yourselves one to another in the fear of God.* [22]*Wives, submit yourselves unto your own husbands, as unto the Lord.* [23]*For the husband is the head of the wife, even as Christ is the head of the Church: and he is the savior of the body.* [24]*Therefore as the Church is subject unto Christ, so let the wives be to their own husbands in every thing.* [25]*Husbands, love your wives, even as Christ also loved the Church and gave himself for it;* [26]*that he may sanctify and cleanse it with the washing of water by the word,* [27]*that he might present it to himself a glorious church, not having spot, or wrinkle, or any such thing; but that it should be holy and without blemish.* [28]*So ought men to love their wives as their own bodies. He that loveth his wife loveth himself.*

HOW TO BE INFLUENTIAL ON THE FAMILY MOUNTAIN

We are called to a life of holiness in every area of our lives. As women, we must submit ourselves to our own husbands as it is fit in the

MANDATE TO INVADE THE 7 MOUNTAINS OF GOD

Lord. God is commanding us to love one another as He loves us. To do otherwise is to conform to the continual destruction of the Family Mountain of God. We must actively nurture our family relationships, and fight for our marriages and our families within our own culture. We have to be born again to possess the wisdom of God that will operate in the lives of our families. We must have God as the head, center and base of our relationships to others. In short, women must be virtuous as the woman described in Proverbs 31.

Males and females were formed to establish families that reflect the glory (magnificence, grace, beauty and majesty) of God. Christ has to be restored as the head of our families. When men and women are equally yoked with our mates, born again and seeking first the Kingdom of God and His righteousness, then He has promised that He adds all other things. The covenant that is made to our Heavenly Father to be obedient to His word and to give Him glory and honor likewise should inspire and sustain the marriage covenant, the vow that is made between a man and a woman in holy matrimony. It should represent and honor God. Having a heart for God's Word helps us to keep our goals in mind and our hearts open to the transformational work of the Holy Spirit in our lives. When we delight to do the will of the Lord, His law is written within our hearts. The word in our hearts helps us to be obedient and grow while He instills within patience and commitment along the way. When this key element (obedience) is in place (which is God the Father), it stabilizes marriages and families.

After the commandment to love the Lord our God with all of our hearts, minds, souls and strength, Jesus said that our next greatest commandment and responsibility is to love one another. A marriage founded on love unconditional is destined for greatness and support from God. Once a connection of love and our oneness with the Father is established, prayer becomes a powerful weapon. Remember that when you pray, believe in faith by touching and agreeing, then you can have what you ask of the Father. Be mindful of the words that you speak to each other and the tones with which those words are conveyed. Words can destroy your marriage or give it the power you and your spouse need to make them stronger in Christ. Some married couples are killing each other with their words, while surrendering their time of prayer to distractions. Or, relationships are fraught with breakdowns in communication, resulting in unloving, unhappy couples, raising confused, angry, and often rebellious children.

As believers, you possess everything needed to make your marriages work, because you love the Lord and are brought together by Him for His purposes. Therefore, try hard to solidify your marriage today more than ever. The enemy has come up against marriages like never before and none of us can afford to keep sleeping and watching the enemy tear families apart. With infidelity steadily on the rise, the eyes of men and women alike are not satisfied. "I want this." "I want that." "I want him." "I want her." Stop! Pray and ask God to help you to be content with what you have and with whom you are sharing your life.

Today, more than ever, we are making choices without seeking Christ, which is causing all types of ungodly behaviors. For example, some mothers are choosing men – or even other women – who come into their lives and harm their children and families. For that matter, we are not training our young women to be lady-like so that they are respected by the young boys in school, church or just at the local hang-outs. We must teach them how to have self-respect and raise their self-esteem levels, so that they become comfortable with who they are within themselves as well as in Christ. Just as importantly, when our young women become secure with who they are, they will not be a target for mistreatment by men or anyone else.

Our young people have to have a deeper understanding as to why they should not have sex before marriage. Oftentimes, premarital sex

MANDATE TO INVADE THE 7 MOUNTAINS OF GOD

opens doors for other ungodly behaviors. Sex is a tool that the enemy will use as power against us. For that reason, young men and women must be made aware that they and the destinies for which God created them are worth more than their temporary, lustful desires.

Fathers must commit to "active" fathering in their families and in the community. They can start by training young men to pull up their pants, pursue higher education and to manifest respectful and respectable behaviors. So, if you teach a young man how to first respect his mother and sisters, there is a strong possibility that he may respect other women as well. Though it may seem that we have lost the battle for our children, they are not beyond our reach. It is going to take unconditional love and the wisdom of God to bring this Mountain of the Family into God's plan for the family. We have to get back to seeking God for everything that concerns us.

One thing that is of definite concern is our iniquity and that it will impact our families. You should know that your iniquities will find you out. 2 Timothy 3:1 says, "This know also, that in the last days perilous times [*full of danger and risk*] shall come" (emphasis mine, 2 Timothy 3:1). What appears to be accepted as freedom of choice or "progressive" thinking that is embodied in the legalization of same sex marriage and granting gay couples the right to adopt children, is abominable to God. Christendom should not make light of what is already put in place by our Lord and Savior Jesus Christ. Our choices affect our children's lives forever.

Christians must own up to the fact that there are other sins/iniquities that are an abomination to God as well. For example, such sins as dishonesty, pride, greed, lust, gluttony, ignoring God's law, living unholy lives, professing to be holy and denying the laws of Christ, are unrighteous behaviors or acts. Sin is sin. We should ALL turn away from ALL things not pleasing to God. If He hates sin, we should also hate sin, but not the person bound by the sin.

Fortunately, some of the damage done to families has nothing to do with the personal choices of a father or a mother, but may have everything to do with the rights of certain government agencies to make on behalf of families. For example, some states' division of child protective services may intervene on the parents' role to raise disciplined, obedient and respectful children. As a result, our children become products of social dysfunction. But with the proper use of these systems, protection and guidance can be provided for those that have a need for it, while maintaining the parents' authority in and over their own homes. As we all seek to raise successful children within our communities, let us be guided by Solomon's wisdom in Proverbs 1:8-25.

> [8]"My son, hear the instruction of thy father, and forsake not the law of thy mother: [9]For they *shall* be on ornament of grace unto thy head, and chains about thy neck [*Children listen when your parents correct you*]. [10]My son, if sinners entice thee, consent thou not [*If your friends ask you to do something that goes against what God's Word or your parent(s) taught you, do not do it*]. [11]If they say, Come with us, let us lay wait for blood, let us lurk privily for the innocent without a cause: [12]Let us swallow them up alive as the grave; and whole, as those that go down into the pit: [13]We shall find all precious substance, we shall fill our houses with spoil: [14]Cast in thy lot among us; let us all have one purse: [15]My son, walk not thou in the way with them; refrain [*remove, turn around*] thy foot from their path: [16]For their feet run to evil, and make haste to shed blood: [17]Surely in vain the net is spread in the sight of any bird]. [18]And they lay wait for their own blood; they lurk privily for their own lives. [19]So *are* the ways of every one that is greedy of gain which taketh away the life of the owners thereof. [20]Wisdom crieth without; she uttereth her voice in the streets. [21]She

MANDATE TO INVADE THE 7 MOUNTAINS OF GOD

crieth in the chief place of concourse, in the openings of the gates: in the city she uttereth her words, *saying*, ²²How long, ye simple ones will ye love simplicity? And the scorners delight in their scorning, and fools hate knowledge? ²³Turn you at my reproof behold, I will pour out my spirit unto you, I will make known my words unto you. ²⁴Because I have called, and ye refused; I have stretched out my hand, and no man regarded]; ²⁵But ye have set at nought all my counsel, and would none of my reproof.

Proverbs 1:26-33 goes on to say,
  ²⁶"I also will laugh at your calamity; I will mock when your fear cometh; ²⁷When your fear cometh as desolation and your destruction cometh as a whirlwind; when distress and anguish cometh upon you. ²⁸Then shall they call upon me, but I will not answer; they shall seek me early, but they shall not find me: ²⁹For that they hated knowledge, and did not choose the fear of the LORD: ³⁰They would none of my counsel: and despised all of my reproof. ³¹Therefore shall they eat of the fruit of their own way, and be filled with their own devices. ³²For the turning away of the simple shall slay them, and the prosperity of fools shall destroy them. ³³But whoso hearkeneth unto me shall dwell safely, and shall be quiet from fear of evil."

It is not wise to live a life that will allow God to turn his back on you; it's not worth it. He wants us to live our lives based on obedience and faith in Him so that in the end we will live with Him forever. We don't want to be told to depart from him because we practiced iniquity.

In the Body of Christ, some simply do not want to confront sin, despite the fact that we are called of God to transform and live by His Spirit. Galatians 5:19-21 speaks of life lived in the flesh rather than lived according to the Spirit of God.

> *Now the works of the flesh are manifest, which are these; adultery, fornication, uncleanness, lasciviousness, idolatry, witchcraft, hatred, variance, emulations, wrath, strife, seditions, heresies, envyings, murders, drunkenness, reveling, and such like: of the which I tell you before, as I have also told you in time past, that they which do such things shall not inherit the kingdom of God.*

At some point in our lives, we all have sinned and fallen short of the Glory of God. The good news is that if we repent (i.e., express sincere remorse) of those things that held us bound, God hears us and forgives us. We can begin again and become the men and women that we were intended to be. By doing this and by exemplifying Christ-like character in our homes, the result will be harmony and peace on the Family Mountain. Men have to seek Christ, then "man up," stand up and take their rightful place in the Kingdom of God. This mountain can exceed at its highest by honoring God's plan for the family. We can do all things through Christ that strengthens us, according to Philippians 4:13. Matthew 11:12 states, "the kingdom of heaven suffers violence and the violent take it by force." Our hearts and minds have to be prepared for aggressive action as we pull down strongholds over our marriages, children and families. We must disarm the "strong man," which is done by discerning and accessing those things in our lives that are not aligning themselves to the Word of God. They are those powerful distractions that no matter what we do, they don't go away. By giving God total pre-eminence over our marriages and families we will live victorious lives in Christ. Psalm 68: 5 tells us, "A father of the fatherless, and a judge of the widows, *is* God in His holy habitation. God setteth the solitary in families: he bringeth out those which are bound with chains: but the rebellious dwell in a dry land." From this, we can see that God even helps those who have no family. Everything that we need is with the One who has already covenanted with all of us.

MANDATE TO INVADE THE 7 MOUNTAINS OF GOD

It is going to take spiritual wisdom, knowledge and understanding to break every chain that binds us to disobedience of our heavenly Father. Nothing should exalt itself as a giant over us because we have the power to overcome our fears and dismantle the tools the enemy uses to bind us. Our commitment to God and to each other has to be solidified in order to move to the next level of being fruitful and multiplying.

When we start having children, we must train them up in the way they should go, so that as they get older they will not depart from the truth, as written in Proverbs 22:6. Children learn from the way their families live; all of their life experiences shape their future. We must do everything in our power to train and raise wholesome children and have joyful family lives. In order to make our homes and home life safe, we must stay in the Word, be obedient to what the Word says about marriage, raise our children in a joyful, peaceful home and diligently seek God. We can no longer let ungodly television programs, movies and videos raise our kids. If we are to advance the Family Mountain, we must first take control of our own homes. Parents, put your foot down and stop letting violent videos poison your children's minds. "For to be carnally minded *is* death; but to be spiritually minded *is* life and peace. Because the carnal mind *is* enmity against God: for it is not subject to the law of God, neither indeed can be" (Romans 8:6). There is enmity when a person is actively against, opposed to or hostile to someone or something. There is palpable hatred or resentment. If you truly want your sons and daughters engaged in warfare, teach them about *spiritual* warfare, a battle that is won in complete victory and without sin and bloodshed. You see, love on Earth has waxed cold and the only way to win our children back from the snare of the enemy is with spiritual warfare and the love of God that lives in our hearts. It's not too late. It is time to cover our children and our children's children with the Blood of Jesus (His sustaining power and Life) and the Word of God.

We have to get back to studying the Word of God to be effective in bringing peace and love to our families. It's important to know what powers we possess in order to know how to use them. With wisdom, knowledge and understanding of what a mighty God we serve, it doesn't matter how messed up we are because we can begin again right now by asking God for forgiveness of past sins, turning back to God, seeking Him with our whole hearts, acknowledging Him in all our ways, and leaning not to our own understanding so that we may receive direction and guidance for training our children and grandchildren. Proverbs 29:15-17 says, "The rod and reproof give wisdom: but a child left to *himself* bringeth his mother to shame. When the wicked are multiplied, transgression increaseth: but the righteous shall see their fall. Correct thy son, and he shall give thee rest; yea, he shall give delight unto thy soul." If we spare the rod we will ruin that child, according to Proverbs 13:24, and when left without discipline, he will cause problems for his parents and problems for himself also. Once children reach a certain age and we recognize that they are without discipline, some become fearful of these kids, but there is good news: God did not give us a spirit of fear but one of power, love and a sound mind to use (2 Timothy 1:7). We have to speak to the spirit in these kids and tell it where to go; you don't have to fear it. Proverbs 19:18,19 instructs us, "Chasten thy son while there is hope, and let not thy soul spare for his crying." That is to say discipline your son and daughter while there is still hope; otherwise, you may ruin their lives.

In closing, I encourage you to choose not the path of destruction, but instead choose the one that leads you to God. Choose life. Instill obedience into your children and to the Lord, for it is the right thing to do. He will be your shield and a very present help in your time of need. Be diligent in seeking God and all His ways. God has a plan for you that is far greater than anything that you could imagine. He plans to prosper you and not harm you. He desires to give you a hope and a future. He keeps you as the apple of His eye.

CHAPTER FOUR

THE EDUCATION MOUNTAIN

Educators | Administration | Curriculum | Medicine
Research | Institutions of Learning

WHAT IS THE EDUCATION MOUNTAIN?

The Education Mountain is one of the strategic mountains of cultural influence. This mountain calls upon the saved to accept the call on their lives to be more than educators. I believe you were set aside by God to bring Kingdom principles to the Education Mountain, walking always in the light of God's words, applying truth at all times and dealing honestly in all things. You are doers of the word not hearers only and you fully understand that Christ is the Head of the body that makes up this mountain.

You may wonder, what do iniquities and immorality have to do with education? When we accepted Christ as our Savior, we became new creatures in Christ and we had to learn to make sure that the old man (the selfish part of who we are) dies daily. The new creature lives and works out salvation by living a life for Christ even in a career in education. Educators are commissioned by God to bring change and influence to a student body of children, setting them on a pathway of success, preparing them for the world around them and giving them the academic and spiritual tools needed for their God-ordained destinies. Educators are also called and appointed to live and act in such a way that positive change is always possible; therefore, walk worthy of the call and blessing of this career that you have been accepted into.

It is so important to be in a school where the head of the school has received Christ also. It will make your job so much easier because you will then have a common goal – the Kingdom and children. Be patient and gentle with each other as you work to establish His Kingdom order in your schools and school systems.

Educators are great and special in the eyes of God. They teach with various teaching styles and produce great results in student achievement. They possess a type of love that flows from the very heart of God. They have the ability to create and instill in children a sense of pride, self-esteem and an attitude that they "can do all things through Christ because He gives them strength" (Philippians 4:13).

HOW TO HAVE INFLUENCE ON THE EDUCATION MOUNTAIN

Ask God for wisdom, knowledge and understanding because each child is different, remembering that you were once children and our hearts were once darkened until you came into the light of God's Word. Now that your hearts are full of the light of God's Word we must shine it in all the dark places of the Education Mountain and walk in its fullness, being doers of the Word and not just hearers of it. Incidentally, God's promise to those who are obedient to Him and do as He has commanded is equal to eternal life (immortality) with Him.

You are given a special power to succeed. Take a bold stand for Christ. Get in your rightful place and do not be afraid because God is with you. Prayer is your key weapon. When one stands alone, one can easily be defeated, but when two believers stand in agreement, God is in the midst of them and their surroundings. A threefold cord cannot easily be broken. Therefore, connect with other educators who know the Lord as Savior and agree with them that all shall be well. Further with a team of you, you will be better able to infiltrate this mountain with God's power and His principles. The window of opportunity to do this and impact the world is now. The lives you change in this season will produce children that are already equipped for the world and their

MANDATE TO INVADE THE 7 MOUNTAINS OF GOD

places in it. Do not be afraid "for God hath not given us a spirit of fear; but of power, and of love, and of a sound mind" (II Tim 1:7). Out of an obedient heart comes favor from our Father and this favor will take you straight to the top of the Education Mountain.

In nearly every school building, the following classes of people make up the work force: administrators; faculty and their own support staff, technological and medical support staff; counselors; custodians, cafeteria and maintenance staff and others. All must work together for the common goal of educating and keeping the student body safe. In their impact on this mountain, everyone will have to deal with children from all walks of life, cultures, backgrounds, and so on.

There is a wave of destruction that has been ordered by Satan to kill, steal and destroy our children. No wonder many of them feel helpless and bullied. Additionally, they face maneuvering through poverty, gangs, drugs, family discord, joblessness and even fear of deportation, if they are immigrants. They are wrestling with teenage pregnancy, rejection, and low self-esteem.

There is rampant lawlessness, but we declare and decree, the devil is a liar! The Body of Christ stands with the children! The educators of our great school systems all over the world that have been ordained by God will be praying for their protection and solace. They will gain the victory by God through the prayers of the righteous. Together, we will pull down the strongholds that exalt themselves as giants over our children. Prayer has to be a top priority. We cannot lean on our own understanding, but rather, we must acknowledge God in all things. He has the plan to prosper us and not to harm us, to give us hope and a future. It is not by chance that you are where you are as an educator. It was ordered and ordained even in your mother's womb. You are a special person called to a special assignment, and that is to bring a Kingdom mindset to systems in need of transformation, in this case, the education system. Again, you are a special people called to a special assignment. The education and knowledge that you have been endowed with, pass it on. If you save one child through what you know, that one can influence one thousand by multiplication of the desire to help others.

The Kingdom of God is at hand, and every second has to count towards positive change for our children, none of whom is beyond God's reach. You must instill in them morals and self-esteem by edification. In turn, they may go out into the world as young women and men of God who behave honestly and with integrity in all things. They are our future doctors, lawyers, nurses, law enforcement and other careers that shape our society.

Children being able to impact others actually starts with you, the educator, and the church community. Together you bring needed change as well as produce unity through your various gifts in the body of Christ. Here is how that same idea is emphasized in the fourth chapter of Ephesians.

> *[1] I therefore, the prisoner of the Lord, beseech you that ye walk worthy of the vocation wherewith you are called, [2] With all lowliness and meekness, with longsuffering, forbearing one another in love; [3] Endeavoring to keep the unity of the Spirit in the bond of peace. [4] There is one body, and one Spirit, even as ye are called in one hope of your calling; [5] One Lord, one faith, and one baptism, [6] One God and Father of all, who is above all, and through all, and in you all. [7] But unto every one of us is given grace according to the measure of the gift of Christ. [8] Wherefore he saith, When he ascended up on high, he led captivity captive, and gave gifts unto men. [9] (Now that he ascended, what is it but that he also descended first into the lower parts of the earth? [10] He that descended is the same also*

MANDATE TO INVADE THE 7 MOUNTAINS OF GOD

that ascended up far above all heavens, that he may fill all things. ¹¹And He gave some, apostles; and some, prophets; and some, evangelists; and some, pastors and teachers; ¹²For the perfecting of the saints, for the work of the ministry, for the edifying of the body of Christ: ¹³Till we all come into the unity of faith, and of the knowledge of the Son of God, unto a perfect man, unto the measure of the stature of the fullness of Christ.

As an educator, you are united with Christ in such a way that the power that works within you gives you victory in all circumstances. When released in faith, this power shines light in all the dark places. Do not be afraid to reveal offenders that bring hurt, harm and danger to the lives of our children. Your goal is to cancel all assignments that have been spoken or sent against them. It is so important to know the power that you possess in order to transform, convert and mature nations. You have to be willing to please and follow God to be able to be effective in bringing change. The transformation of the Education Mountain must be characterized by the fruit of the spirit which is love, joy, peace, patience, kindness, goodness, faithfulness, gentleness, self-control, meekness and temperance. Those not influenced by your character may remain unchanged, unconverted, and not transformed will continue to be vulnerable to impurity, sexual immortality, idolatry, witchcraft, hatred, discord, jealousy, fits of rage, dissension and selfish ambitions.

As long as the Father's seed remains in you, you live and grow as His plan intends. It is only when that seed is uprooted that His presence is diminished. When God's glory is present we are taught to discern between what is holy and what is profane.

When you take your rightful place in His kingdom, He will reveal to you His vision and His plan for the various mountains of culture that we are to enter. Whenever we as believers seek to honor God's word by seeking out others with Kingdom mindsets, He gives us eyes to discern between good and evil, holy and unholy things (Ezekiel 44:23). When you meet many others that you will minister to, they will know you are not fake and that they are in the very presence of God by His Spirit.

Even though prayer was taken out of the schools, it was not taken out of you. So do not hesitate to use this priceless weapon of warfare. Pray that you do not fall into the trap of falsifying documents that could possibly bring you embarrassment, shame, financial ruin or even prison time, and make your students believe that cheating is okay. You must be an example of a strong leader with no margin for dishonesty. In turn, children will enjoy school, respect authority and learn well under good strong leadership.

It is important to have the Kingdom mindset, so you will use your authority and take control of your classroom and school building. You have been given power and authority over your classroom and building. Therefore any spirits that try to gain controlling access to disrupt your classroom, causing all kinds of disturbance and distractions, will have to flee on your command. However, as difficult as things may get, it is important that you control your space with a loving heart towards the children while at the same time speaking with authority that demands respect. Because the children come from all walks of life you have to make a great impact on their lives in order to make a difference in their lives. The change that you make just might make a difference in their homes. All we can do is try to win as many as can be won for the sake of the Gospel of Jesus Christ. Never become discouraged.

In closing, you are special and a key, hands-on person in sowing the seeds of great knowledge that can come only by the education that you provide for each student. You are very special in the eyes of our Father, Jesus Christ. As a mother and a grandparent, I applaud you because I realize how difficult teaching can be. I also know that you can

MANDATE TO INVADE THE 7 MOUNTAINS OF GOD

accomplish great things with God's plan for your life, if you accept Him and His will for your life. You will be destined for greatness, standing out with your teaching concepts and strategic ways of conveying knowledge and fostering understanding to the students day by day.

Be encouraged by and in the Word of God. You have within reach our future educators, doctors, lawyers, judges, nurses, ministers, counselors (and maybe even a nation's leader!), just to name a few. You can do it! We, your sisters and brothers in Christ, stand with you in prayer to enforce the will of God on the Education Mountain.

CHAPTER FIVE

THE ARTS & ENTERTAINMENT MOUNTAIN

Film | Television | Theatre | Social Media | Music | Dance
Sports | Fashion | Artisans

WHAT IS THE ARTS AND ENTERTAINMENT MOUNTAIN?

When an entertainment company is formed, there is a corporate culture that consists of by-laws and practices that will dictate how that company will be run When we use our talents and our gifts in the entertainment industry, we come under the influence of these practices and bylaws. Therefore we must go into these establishments with our spiritual eyes and ears open, sensitive to the Word of God, because a lot of our entertainment entities may create products which violate the principles of God. We should always remember that we are in this world but not of it (John 17:16), and to condone unrighteousness is to violate the Word of God. "He is the Rock, his work is perfect: for all his ways are judgment: a God of truth and without iniquity, just and right is he," according to Deuteronomy 32:4.

Let us look at visual art (paintings, sculptures, photographs and motion pictures) as a form of communication that conveys a message. Art is a powerful medium that can lead to worship of something or someone. Art has the power to capture the attention, imagination and hearts of people. Our Father God is the greatest Artist and Creator of all time.

¹In the beginning God created the heaven and the earth.
²And the earth was without form, and void; and darkness was upon the face of the deep. And the Spirit of God moved upon the

MANDATE TO INVADE THE 7 MOUNTAINS OF GOD

face of the waters. ³And God said, let there be light: and there was light. ⁴And God saw the light and it was good: and God divided the light from the darkness. ⁵And God called the light Day, and the darkness He called Night. And the evening and the morning were the first day (Genesis 1:1-5).

HOW TO BE INFLUENTIAL ON THE ARTS AND ENTERTAINMENT MOUNTAIN

If you are called to the mountain of Arts and Entertainment, and as you capture your audience, convey your creativity with and through the light of God's Word. Choose to honor Him in all that you do. Your skills and craftsmanship are already in your DNA.

Artisan crafting – highly skilled craftsmanship in some type of art, such as cabinetry, brick masonry, welding of silver and gold, cutting of stone and cloth, or even cooking – is used in the design, manufacturing and promotion of everyday products. God's only request is that we use our gifts, talents and skills to glorify Him. In the book of Exodus, we discover how God chose those He had gifted in the art of tailoring to create the holy garments that His priests would wear for worship in His tabernacle. In Exodus 28:1-3, we read the commandment God gave Moses concerning the make and design of the priestly garments.

> *And take thou unto thee Aaron thy brother, and his sons with him, from among the children of Israel, that he may minister unto me in the priest's office, even Aaron, Nadab and Abihu, Eleazar and Ithamar, Aaron's sons. And thou shalt speak unto all that are wise hearted, whom I have filled with the spirit of wisdom, that they may make Aaron's garments to consecrate him that he may minister unto me in the priest's office.*

There are many professions within the arts and entertainment industry as acting, dance, basketball, football, or modelling. But know that the ability to do all of these things come from the Father and He has a plan to use them for His glory. If you're born again, the Arts and Entertainment Mountain becomes your marketplace, workplace and MINISTRY. We cannot fathom the amount of God's power and grace that He has given you to bring change to these mountains. Those called to this Mountain will clearly produce art by the knowledge of the Voice of the Ultimate Artist, and He will make your way prosperous if you obey Him.

God has placed you in the entertainment industry to help bridge gaps, to make known His unconditional love and His infinite forgiveness, and to help heal the brokenhearted and to set captives free. We have to realize what is acceptable and unacceptable on the mountains of our service. Consider how your walk will impact God's kingdom.

There are role models; there are change agents. These are individuals who should shine their light in the dark places of the entertainment industry. There are many young boys and girls that see performances of their favorite actors, singers and athletes. These children watch everything that some of these performers do and sometimes emulate them. They take notice of the way they dance and perform both on and off the stage, the field, the basketball court, and so on. The point is this: When God promotes you to a level where all eyes are on you, let your behavior be pleasing to God and let it help to change and impact a child's life in a good way. Our children's lives are affected by every positive – and negative – thing they see in our culture. They seek to emulate both the adults in their lives whom they know, and others they observe on television, in movies and in social media outlets every day. Some children emulate what they see others live or portray, whether good or evil.

As with any other mountain of God, people operating on the mountain of arts and entertainment risk falling deeper and deeper into

MANDATE TO INVADE THE 7 MOUNTAINS OF GOD

lawlessness, if they turn away from God and His Word. In my opinion, the secular music industry has become so corrupt that it is primarily about selling sex. Men and women are exploiting their bodies and defiling their temples for money and fame. Further I feel that there are a lot of entertainers who do not reverence God because they want to maintain their level of success. Matthew 16:26 poses a sobering question to what I call selling out to lawlessness. "For what is a man profited, if he shall gain the whole world, and lose his own soul? or what shall a man give in exchange for his soul?"

Seeking to please people rather than God opens doors that are hard to close. Is it any wonder that some of our most well-known "superstars" are struggling with alcohol and drug addictions, depression, and turmoil in their family life? As long as God is the focus of one's life, He will open doors no one can close, and close doors no one can open. But this will only happen as those in this industry seek to please Him through salvation and honoring His commands.

Along with salvation come occupation, career and marketplace responsibilities. Our job as Kingdom change-agents is to shine the light of God's Word in all the dark places of our society, never being afraid to speak truth. We enter into our occupations to stand out for Christ, not to blend in with sin. We are ordained by God, sent by God and should make it our business to be obedient to God. The Holy Spirit is our guide. He speaks as an oracle of God, as indicated in Isaiah 2:2-5.

> *[2]And it shall come to pass in the last days, that the mountain of the Lord's house shall be established in the top of the mountains, and shall be exalted above the hills; and all nations shall flow unto it. [3]And many people shall go and say, Come ye, and let us go up to the mountain of the Lord, to the house of the God of Jacob; and he will teach us of his ways, and we will walk in his paths: for out of Zion shall go*

forth the law, and the word of the Lord from Jerusalem. ⁴And he shall judge among the nations, and shall rebuke many people: and they shall beat their swords into plowshares, and their spears into pruning hooks: nation shall not lift up sword against nation, neither shall they learn war any more. ⁵O house of Jacob, come ye, and let us walk in the light of the Lord.

I believe that it is very challenging for Christian artists to keep their salvation intact in the face of such a demanding work experience that keeps them in the lime light. Finding and befriending people who are saved and plan to stay that way is key to survival. Being a doer of the Word, not a hearer only is also vital. Even though our actors, models and sports stars are only a part of the Hollywood arena, we need Godly film-makers, producers and change agents for the Kingdom of God.

We must be completely transformed, converted and matured in the Word of God. All the things that we have sown into will soon manifest themselves. Whether good or evil, whether we walked in light or darkness, it will manifest. Let us be men and women of integrity and honesty, not lovers of ourselves but lovers of God and of the people of God. I John 1:5-7 states, "This then is the message which we have heard of him, and declare unto you, that God is light, and in him is no darkness at all. If we say that we have fellowship with him, and walk in darkness, we lie, and do not the truth: But if we walk in the light, as he is in the light, we have fellowship one with another, and the blood of Jesus Christ his Son cleanseth us from all sin."

When we walk in God's light, we are filled with wisdom, knowledge and understanding. With understanding we move away from ungodly art forms. At all times, we must stand for what is decent and right. We must honor Him in all things and in all of our ways. Let's help save our nation from destruction. Ezekiel 18:26-32 says,

²⁶When a righteous man turneth away from his

MANDATE TO INVADE THE 7 MOUNTAINS OF GOD

> *righteousness, and committeth iniquity, and dieth in them; for his iniquity that he hath done shall he die. ^{27}Again, when the wicked man turneth away from his wickedness that he hath committed, and doeth that which is lawful and right, he shall save his soul alive. ^{28}Because he considereth, and turneth away from all his transgressions that he hath committed, he shall surely live, he shall not die. ^{29}Yet saith the house of Israel, The way of the Lord is not equal. O house of Israel, are not my ways equal? are not your ways unequal? ^{30}Therefore I will judge you, O house of Israel, every one according to his ways, saith the Lord GOD. Repent, and turn yourselves from all your transgressions; so iniquity shall not be your ruin. ^{31}Cast away from you all your transgressions; whereby ye have transgressed; and make you a new heart and a new spirit: for why will ye die, O house of Israel? ^{32}For I have no pleasure in the death of him that dieth, saith the Lord GOD: wherefore turn yourselves, and live ye.*

On this and every other mountain, our only purpose is to win souls for the Kingdom and to bring glory to God. Therefore, those called to this mountain should not lose sight of their purpose. For starters, they can begin by worshiping the Creator and not the creation. By lifting their hearts in awe of the creation God made, they should give thanks. Secondly, they should remember that God wants all men and women, boys and girls alike, to come to repentance and not to perish eternally. The light and love given to those chosen for this mountain is a love and light that does not have to be forced upon anyone but instead walked in and revealed through a Godly lifestyle. For He gives you gifts that you may stir them up and have wonderful careers on this mountain. While some are blessed with an abundant life, they compromise and forget about our Savior and His purpose for choosing them to take this mountain. If God has chosen you, remember it is not happenstance that you are where you are!

Arts and entertainment should reflect and embody everything that says our Creator is majestic in all things. Therefore, we should be deliberate in the ways we celebrate the creativity given to us in arts, music, fashion and sports as well as in the ways that we are entertained. This reflection should manifest in praise and thanksgiving to the Most High God. In art, create pictures that depict the God-given beauty of the objects represented.

In music, be mindful of the music that flows from within you. Play and sing with the desire to please your primary audience, your heavenly Father, not compromising to please the world instead.

If you are called to the world of sports, strive to good sportsmanship, and be honorable to God and the fans who look up to you, for it is God who has graciously given all these gifts.

In allowing God to take you to higher heights and deeper depths in Him, you will find the more excellent way. Then you can clearly see the plan He has for you, to prosper us and not harm us, to give us hope and a future (Jeremiah 29:11). In this way you develop a Kingdom mindset to reverence God in every way. He truly becomes your focus in bringing change to this mountain.

In this mountain, embrace the beauty of the creativity that God has given to you. Create beauty with the light that is within you for the glory of God. With God, all that you do will stand out in praise to God. Whether on the basketball or tennis courts, on the field, on stage, on canvas, you are to express your God-given talent. And in your expression, there will God be also. So desire the most excellent way by seeking and embracing your vocation with the Kingdom mindset required to please God. Work out your salvation with fear and trembling, reverencing God and not mankind. Respect CEO's, movie studio and record company executives and other high-ranking officials,

MANDATE TO INVADE THE 7 MOUNTAINS OF GOD

but do not conform to the evils that they may stand for. Listen to God's voice and you will make the right decisions concerning our fellow man that will place you in key positions of influence to take this mountain. As workers in this Mountain, know that the earth is the Lord's and everything in it belongs to God. You, me and everything. Everything means everything.

Finally, in using the creativity He placed within you, be assured that you can do all things through Christ that strengthens you as you attempt to be influential on this mountain. Remember that you are that bright light of glory that our Father has released to this mountain to help bring change. You are very well equipped with full armor, grace, and mercy. Share His glory in ways that will inspire others to want the light of God working in their lives. Ask God for strategic ways to release His love, His light, and His glory. So, I say to you, "Let His glory rise within you…take the Mountain!"

CHAPTER SIX

THE BUSINESS MOUNTAIN

Corporations (for-profit and non-profit) | Sole proprietorships
Limited liability partnerships | Limited Liability corporations

A business is an industry or an organization which is involved in commerce (trading products and/or services) to customers. Businesses are especially prevalent in capitalist societies in which wealth is chiefly gained and maintained by private individuals or corporations rather than state-owned or cooperative institutions. A business may also be a "non-profit" or "state owned." A "company" is a business owned by several individuals. Business can relate to a particular organization or an entire market. When money is a major factor in the trade and commerce of an organization, it is referred to as business. The common denominator in all businesses is money or the owners', boards of directors' or investors' desire to profit from that business. There are many facets of ownership, such as sole proprietorship, partnership, corporation, and co-op. They fall either under limited liability or unlimited liability designations.
(Retrieved from the internet August 12, 2017, 12:59PM. https://en.wikiquote.org/wiki/Capitalism*)*

WHAT IS THE BUSINESS MOUNTAIN OF GOD?

Here are a few principles at the working of any business. First, bylaws are in place to determine how that company will be run. Next, that company's level of efficiency is determined by how it utilizes its resources (including human resources), as well as the efficiency of marketing plans, production strategies and its operations management.

MANDATE TO INVADE THE 7 MOUNTAINS OF GOD

As I stipulated earlier, human resources are a vital part of a company's administration. The hiring and training of all personnel is key to a company's success and longevity. Employees should be selected because of strong knowledge and/or skills related to the position and their ability to perform effectively consistently.

Careful consideration should be taken when selecting leaders for your company. Strong motivation and management skills will no doubt help the morale of your company which will result in an enthusiastic team with the desire to reach and exceed industry standards.

In the case of small businesses, how well you set up your business determines its potential for success. Like all other businesses, a small business must be built with integrity and morals and not simply an owner's greed for personal gain. We've heard it said that "Business is business," particularly from people who want to give themselves permission to treat employees and even customers poorly. But the actual truth is that Kingdom-minded business owners must found their businesses on Godly principles. I believe to be effective in any business you must have a heart full of God's love. This ensures that all employees are treated with respect and consideration, and that they will be paid good salaries so that adequate provisions will be made for them and their families.

When you enter into the Business Mountain, the best equipment that you can possess is salvation. Then you are really equipped to succeed and run a successful business. Being born again gives you access to a Kingdom mindset and the Godly principles needed to operate in the plan that God has for your life. Jeremiah 29:11-13 states, "For I know the thoughts I think towards you, saith the Lord, thoughts of peace, and not of evil, to give you an expected end. Then ye shall call upon me, and ye shall go and pray unto me, and I will hearken unto you. And ye shall seek me, and find me, when ye shall search for me with all your heart." Therefore, as a believer in Christ, you have to have the love of Christ in your heart because you will need patience, love, compassion, and integrity for your employees that partake in the success of our business. Therefore, a relationship with God is imperative in establishing core values within your business. In doing so, you will become known as a Christian company. Just as Jesus told Peter in Matthew 16:18, "...upon this rock I will build my church; and the gates of hell shall not prevail against it," so it is and will be with the business you establish with the Father as your business leader.

When you have a Kingdom mindset in business, you are given God's abiding love which helps us to grow in grace. You become matured, transformed and converted business men and women. You must know the voice of God in order to hear Him when He speaks to us. His voice you will learn is the only voice that will lead and guide you to a peace that will surpass all understanding. Not knowing the voice of God when He's speaking to you can set you up for unnecessary struggles in your quest to do things your way. Kingdom mindset leaders are doers of the word not just hearers. Without a Kingdom mindset, your business will not function as well because you will be operating without the benefits of God's grace and wisdom, and you will run the risk of being out of the will or perhaps the timing of God as you make important decisions about the future of your business. When you approach business as representatives of Christ in the marketplace at large, God gives us a discerning spirit to foresee and recognize trouble and the tricks of the enemy ahead of time. Matthew 24:24 lets us know, "If it is possible, the very elect will be deceived." Kingdom mindset men and women that are walking in their destiny will attract others that are like them in spirit and in ethics. One thing I know for sure after 29 years of business ownership: If you don't know Christ and are not established in your walk with Him, the school of hard knocks will knock you down. But a good man will fall seven times and he can still get up every time in Christ, because He promised never to leave us or forsake us. He never

MANDATE TO INVADE THE 7 MOUNTAINS OF GOD

said that weapons would not form against you, but He did promise they would not ultimately destroy you. For example, suppose you experience a fire. Your business burns and through no fault of your own, you lack necessary coverage. This happened to me many years ago. The lesson I learned from that experience was TRUST. My former insurance company made a hard-hearted, cold, "business" decision against me. I didn't have *insurance*, but God used this opportunity to show me that my assurance was in Him and all I needed to do was have faith and trust Him. I was in a situation that I had no control over, nor did I have the power to change it. BUT GOD re-established my business in two months. I was blessed with a brand new, fully-equipped salon, and he added nine new operators to help me build it. So, I personally know that having the Kingdom mindset in business, as well as on the other mountains, is the only way to succeed. Having Kingdom mindsets and doing things God's way is the only way that He can work through us to bring light to the dark places that hold people captive and oppressed. As a Christin business owner, it becomes your duty to build on Godly principles outlined in God's Word. Your trust in God has to be steadfast so that others may become inspired with that same trust. It may not always be easy, but I do know that when you don't know what to do, don't make a move. Hold on to the revelation that God can and will do above and beyond all that you could ever ask or think. His guidance is great and real; wait on the Lord. He may not answer you or eliminate the problem right away, but He will come through for you and your business. This is why you must always treat employees and customers with love and honor, having no respect of persons (the tendency to prefer one over another based on superficial appearances or ideas). Micah 6:8 shows us, "He hath showed thee, O man, what is good; and what doth the Lord require of thee, but to do justly, and to love mercy, and to walk humbly with thy God?" God's grace is sufficient for all who want to receive it. Isaiah 1:17-19 declares, "Learn to do well; seek judgment, relieve the oppressed, judge the fatherless, plead for the widow. Come now, and let us reason together, saith the Lord: though your sins be as scarlet, they will be as white as snow; though they be red like crimson, they shall be as wool." If you develop the type of heart that God desires for us, you will be loyal to your employees, your customers and all those you meet in the course of delivering your goods and services daily. Every type of business imaginable exists upon on this planet. The type of business you choose does not so much matter as does the intent of your heart. Because you have accepted Christ as your personal savior, then allow Him to develop within you a Kingdom mindset that will not only transform your business but will also transform you in such a way that people will be drawn to Christ. Surely, this is a Christian business owner's most reasonable service.

Becoming a Kingdom mindset leader, knowing the laws of Godly principles as well as business laws, having accountability in business, showing fiscal responsibility, and possessing solid operations knowledge and flow are all necessary criteria for running a successful business. Never compromise your Godly principles for quick gains in a company. It will prove to be unworthy of the sacrifice.

As you develop a Kingdom mindset in running your business, you will attract employees who respect your outlook. They will appreciate and mimic your attitude and behavior. They will understand their purpose for being employed by your business. They will enter into a healthy relationship with their colleagues as well as management. In turn, your business will manifest the success and the glory of God Himself. Doors will open for you to testify of why your business is such a success and you will share the ideas behind "Kingdom Business." Others will come to know and understand the Kingdom mindset, which carries with it the understanding that making money is not the only reason to enter into business. They will see that God ordained Godly business to shine the light and love of God into the dark places of the earth. They will know that God has not called them to take advantage of people in business, but to labor for Christ and not just the company.

MANDATE TO INVADE THE 7 MOUNTAINS OF GOD

If you are reading this book, you may be a Christian already. So, I do not think it is far reaching for me to think that you already know that all you do should be done for the glory of God. By now you probably realize that hosting the Presence of God in your business will make all the difference in the world, particularly as it relates to fostering godly attitudes among employees, such as love, respect and unity. In so doing, this will have a tremendous positive impact on your company's morale.

Understandably, perhaps not all who come in contact with you will be born again, but it is possible that if you consider your workplace your ministry, it opens up an opportunity for precious souls to become saved. Remember that just as old, unproductive workplace habits were formed, they can also be broken by the renewing of your ways. A good start can be determining to bring the peace of God to every situation, every person that you encounter, and loving all of your neighbors – the people you come in contact with every day – even though you may not initially receive it in return.

In the event you are an employee, then do not take your employment for granted. After all, it is God Who favored you to get the job and who has placed you on assignment there. Look at your employment as an opportunity to display God's love, oh how wonderful things will be. God's love and unity always bring needed change. Think about I Thessalonians 5:11-13, "Wherefore comfort yourselves together, and edify one another, even as also ye do. And we beseech you, brethren, to know them which labor among you, and are over you in the Lord, and admonish you; And to esteem them very highly in love for their work's sake. And be at peace among yourselves."

Kingdom mindsets come with obedience, love, patience, kindness, gentleness, choices, truth, integrity, wisdom, knowledge, and understanding. Deuteronomy 8:18 puts it this way: "But thou shalt remember the Lord thy God: for it is he that giveth thee power to get wealth, that he may establish his covenant which he sware unto thy fathers, as it is this day."

Whether you are a business owner or an employee, follow God's plan for your life. God has action plans for you to live a life pleasing to Him without compromise. It is a life of value, favor, integrity, giving of ourselves, and doing well for others. You should be so in tuned with His Holy Spirit that you trust Him with every aspect of your life
    Finally, operate your businesses with faith, integrity, and love for all people. Even in the world of business, everybody is somebody to Christ.

CHAPTER SEVEN

THE GOVERNMENT MOUNTAIN

Local government | State government | National government
Military branches | Laws and Policies | Lobbyists
Ambassadors to the nations

For unto us a child is born, unto us a son is given: and the government shall be upon his shoulder: and his name shall be called Wonderful, Counsellor, The mighty God, The everlasting Father, the Prince of Peace. Of the increase of his government and peace there shall be no end, upon the throne of David, and upon his kingdom, to order it, and to establish it with judgment and with justice from henceforth even forever and ever. The zeal of the Lord of hosts will perform this.
(Isaiah 9:6-7)

WHAT IS THE GOVERNMENT MOUNTAIN OF GOD?

Government. What is government? It is any political institution that establishes order. In the United States of America, our governmental system consists of the national, local and state governments, military, law and policy, lobbyists, ambassadors and social services. These are some of the many entities that fall within our governmental system. These parts were intended to function and rule our nation as well as to administer civil service and justice on all levels in government.

The Government Mountain is a widespread field that expands far. The President is placed high in this mountain, along with others that are selected to help make up his administrative team. In our country, the

President is the physical person at the top of this mountain and is often seen in many ways, such as head of state (aka, head of the government), the chief executive, chief administrator, chief diplomat, commander-in-chief, chief legislator, party chief and chief citizen, just to name a few. While the president is the symbol of our government, governors, senators and representatives are also placed in authoritative positions. Sadly, some of our politicians are using their positions to enrich themselves, oppress others and are taking part in all types of corruption that violate the principles of God as outlined in the Scriptures. Many, in my opinion, have also violated the trusts and interests of those whom they represent.

God has a plan for the future of government to prosper it and not to bring harm, to give us a hope and a future. Without a vision we will perish. All suffer when there is no vision, as there is no guidance or moral standards by which to be governed. Due to a lack of vision, problems arise because the opposing sides of our American political system seem to lack both principle and purpose for governing everyone. They oppose the viable solutions to the problems that plague us. This conduct is not conducive to our nation's success and it produces more discord and greater willingness to compromise godly standards.

Many elected officials use influence and power to obtain wealth for themselves and their friends, while the poor remain poor and the middle class continues a downward slide. Unfortunately, through manipulation, pride and deception, the enemy has held some of our greatest elected officials captive to all types of political and personal corruption. There was a time in our nation's history that even though two persons may have found themselves at opposite ends of the spectrum on a given political or social issue, they still managed to communicate and behave themselves in a respectful and civil way. That no longer appears to be the case. For instance, when our nation elected the first African-American man to hold the office of President, there was

MANDATE TO INVADE THE 7 MOUNTAINS OF GOD

a tremendous amount of venomous disrespect and even political sabotage. In my opinion, this seemed to embolden many other elected officials and some of the citizenry to outwardly speak against President Obama and everything that he was trying to do for the people of this great nation in a very disturbing and harmful way. Let the record show, no matter the person's race, gender, or culture, all leaders deserve respect – and even double honor when they serve well.

The vision to govern is very vital with respect to our core values. A lot of leaders begin with a genuine desire to help or to make people's lives better when they begin to govern, but then once they are voted into office, they seem to quickly forget the promises they made to the people and the important issues in our society (healthy families, good jobs, safe neighborhoods, equal access to education, morally correct entertainment, accountability, etc.). To whom much is given, much is required. This political pattern must be broken and dismantled in order to bring peace and justice to the Government Mountain the way God intended. In order to avoid social breakdowns that contribute to lawlessness, social unrest, violence and all types of debauchery, our government has to be credible, purposeful, and forthcoming in truth-telling in order to hold our society together in peace and love for the common good.

Great leadership on the Government Mountain is a vital part of our culture. To degrade or diminish any necessary element of the government makes our culture weak and unstable. Our culture is weakened further by corrupt leadership that does not live by Godly values. Corrupt leaders and politicians must realize that "we the people" will no longer accept self-serving, greedy actions from them. We have lost a lot by way of men and women in government that were put into positions for which they were not qualified; some even paid bribes to get into office.

When we look at the national debt which is in the trillions of dollars, and the many careless ways that some of our former leaders handled their positions, our only hope is to turn back to God whom we can trust. Our trust in our leaders has been compromised and we must turn back to God and ask that "He plant compassion, prayer, love, wisdom, knowledge, understanding and patience deep within our hearts. These things are key if we are to be effective in finding solutions to all the issues that pertain to the Government Mountain" (retrieved from the internet, *http://www.7culturalmountains.org/apps/articles/default.asp?articleid=39113&columnist, July 7, 2017, 2:41PM*).

With our faith, we can believe that everything will work together for the good for those that love the Lord and are called according to His purpose. We know and have an understanding that our steps are ordered by God. Our knowledge of Him tells us He will never leave us nor forsake us. In our prayers to Him, we see His faithfulness to fulfill and perfect all that concerns us. The prayers of the righteous avail much. We understand that when we attempt to influence this mountain, we must let the love of God shine bright in our hearts. In building our relationships with others, we need the compassion and the patience from our Father's heart to be able to help others. We must learn how to walk and work with others; we are the children of the Most High God. We are in this world but not of this world. God has equipped us with Kingdom mindsets to obey Him and to establish his Kingdom principles wherever we may live, so that our godliness is not comprised. Isaiah 9:6,7 declare, "For unto us a child is born, unto us a son is given: and the government shall be upon his shoulder: and his name shall be called Wonderful, Counsellor, The mighty God, The everlasting Father, the Prince of Peace. Of the increase of his government and peace there shall be no end, upon the throne of David, and upon his kingdom, to order it, and to establish it with judgment and with justice from henceforth even forever. The zeal of the Lord of hosts will perform this."

MANDATE TO INVADE THE 7 MOUNTAINS OF GOD

HOW TO HAVE INFLUENCE ON THE GOVERNMENT MOUNTAIN

If you are called to the Government Mountain, please know that it is required of you to address and change all things that do not work for the good of the people under any current state of government. One of the main things you must do is to know those who are laboring with you. Those in Christ with the Kingdom mindset know full on that they don't have to be forceful or bully their way to be seen as great leaders, because these leaders are humbly led by God to greatness. Godly leaders pray before entering into meetings by pulling down strongholds that hold minds captive; they do not operate in the flesh. God's guidance helps them to administer wisdom by solving problems with great expertise and He gives them Godly strategies with signs following. Exodus 31:6 tells us, "and behold, I have given with him Aholiab, the son of Ahisamach, of the tribe of Dan. And in the hearts of all that are wise hearted I have put wisdom, that they may make all that I have commanded thee." Our government leaders must begin to create atmospheres and strategies that are designed to help men and women to succeed in the workplace, to create great jobs here in the United States that cannot be outsourced to other countries, to spark wage increases, to make education more affordable for all who wish to obtain it, or to ensure equal rights for ALL people, regardless of race, gender, age, disability, and so on. "We the People" are simply asking for leadership to do right for the people and by the people. In our recent history, some of our leaders understood that everyone deserves a fair chance and the poor will always be among us, therefore we now have in place affordable health care granted to those that were sick and could not afford sometimes life-saving treatments and medications. Though the plan had certain challenges and pitfalls, there are quantified millions of lives on the line if the Act is overthrown with no sensible, valid replacement. It is a sobering thought indeed. If our lawmakers do not do the right thing, people could literally die.

To those on this mountain, God is saying "Fear not." Because of your wisdom, you are equipped to succeed. You, as Kingdom men and women, are equipped spiritually, emotionally and intellectually for this call to serve God's people and you will flourish on every side. You are just as ordained to serve in government, as a pastor is to pastor a church. You are endowed with God's Spirit to bring the government of God down to earth. Seek as much knowledge as you can both spiritually and intellectually, for knowledge is power. God loves you so much that He has set in you His heart's desire for government. You are His choice for service to His people. You are His anointed; serve Him as you serve His people. Be committed, steadfast, uncompromising, loving, gentle, kind, longsuffering and patient. Learn, listen to and obey the voice of God.

In Kingdom leadership there has to be a deep-seated desire to please and obey God. Just as you trust God, He must be able to trust you also. Learn to yield yourself more and more to God so that you truly become the Kingdom of God in a government ordained by God. When our God trusts our leaders, there is nothing that He will withhold from them. He promises to open doors no man can shut. Therefore if you are called to this mountain, God trusts you to make decisions of every type, scope and magnitude. Even though you make mistakes, He will still stand with you. A righteous man may fall seven times or seventy times, but he will rise again EVERY time (Proverbs 24:16). It doesn't matter what level of government you work in, walk in the Godly call to govern that is on your life. Be committed to stand against corruption, bribery and all opposition to the will of God. In short, the required standards for leadership on this mountain are the fear of God, an intimate relationship with Him, and to be a man or woman after God's own heart.

Our culture is weakened when governmental leadership is corrupt, and leaders neglect God's ethics. Those who have governed in this way

MANDATE TO INVADE THE 7 MOUNTAINS OF GOD

must understand that no longer will their self-serving and greedy ways be accepted. We as a people have lost so much at the hands of some leaders in government who were placed in positions that they were not qualified for

As a consequence of corruption by some who operate on this mountain, many American citizens no longer trust this institution that was actually ordained by God Himself. How can a leader on this mountain expect to be respected and trusted when he or she is doing corruptible things?

To our men and women in uniform who patrol our cities, what is it about law enforcement that makes you think that you are above the law? If you are in authority, and your own behavior it is illegal and immoral, this is called an abuse of authority. Here we are in 21st century with men and women in positions of authority abusing their power by ways of compromise and doing things that displease the Father. There has been an increase in senseless killings, bullying, greed and brutality against citizens across our country and not much is being done about it.

To some of our lawmakers, how long will you sleep and turn a deaf ear?

To our judicial system that is responsible for righteous judgment, how long will you ruin the lives of the innocent while convicted felons are released from prison to roam freely and do additional harm to others?

Peace has to prevail, and it must start within our government. I beg of you to lay aside every hindrance that keeps you from walking in the calling that has been placed in your life that you might be of service to this great nation. We as the Body of Christ stand with you and your families to keep you protected and lifted up to our God, the Author and Finisher of our faith.

We must open our minds and our ears and oppose all new laws that will lead us to consequences that threaten what we know to be morally correct. We have to obey the truth of God's words, the Ten Commandments of life. These laws were given to Moses for us to live by. The world as we see it today is on this watered-down wave, which means everything that has influenced us to live a life for Christ has somehow been weakened by a system put in place to renounce the mere existence of God and mock Him in everything. But God has commanded us to do good unto all men, especially those of the household of faith. If you continue to suppress and sabotage people's lives, you set up for yourselves generational curses that will continue to be passed down through your lineage. The consequences of your sins may fall on your children and your children's children. The good news is you can, wherever you are, take up the cross and follow Jesus. You can humble yourselves and pray, turn from your wicked ways, and God will hear from heaven and heal our land. Get wisdom, get knowledge and get understanding.

There is a new nation that God is raising up that will obey Him. These are those with Kingdom mindsets who will do God's will on earth as it is in heaven. These new Kingdom mindset leaders will be established in every nation and culture, united by the effectual prayers of the saints of God, and not by political influence alone. The Kingdom mindset leader is put in office from intercessory prayers. We, the Body of Christ, with the voice of our leadership, will cry out to God in Heaven for all His leaders to emerge to the forefront and dismantle the opposers speedily. Daniel 2:21-22 declares, "And he changeth the times and the seasons: he removeth kings, and setteth up kings: he giveth wisdom unto the wise, and knowledge to them that know understanding: he revealeth the deep and secret things: he knoweth

MANDATE TO INVADE THE 7 MOUNTAINS OF GOD

what is in the darkness, and the light dwelleth with him." Turn now unto Him and serve the people you were placed in government to serve. It's not your government but God's government established to serve and to protect His people.

You must be a doer of the word not a hearer only. You must have no fear because God didn't give you a spirit of fear but one of power, love and a sound mind. Therefore, you have the ability to be wise, knowledgeable, and understanding while also trusting in the Lord with all your heart and not to lean to your own understanding.

With God's holy armor, those called to the Government Mountain can stand against any and all of the wiles of the enemy (Satan). Ephesians 6 admonishes us to be assured that this is a spiritual battle against wickedness in high places, not a battle against flesh and blood. We should speak truth always and keep the breastplate of righteousness upon us. We are told that the shield of faith will quench every fiery dart or attack from the wicked one. As we wear the helmet of salvation and wield with proficiency the Sword of the Spirit which is the Word of God, we should always pray, persevering for the saints. We must all remember that we are called to serve and not simply to be served. Humility is key. He promised to give grace to the humble. Remember also that a Kingdom mindset is essential, and you do not have to wear a sign stating who you are, for you have a special light that wise men will see and take note.

CONCLUDING THOUGHTS

I pray that in some way you have obtained a better understanding of these incredible mountains and how they relate to you within our culture and the Kingdom of God. By endeavoring to acquire a Kingdom mindset, you will develop a heart like God's own heart.
In order to keep ourselves free from becoming entangled with iniquities that will cause us to stumble. Hebrews 12:1-2 states, "Wherefore seeing we also are compassed about with so great a cloud of witnesses, let us lay aside every weight, and the sin which doth so easily beset us, and let us run with patience the race that is before us, looking unto Jesus the author and finisher of our faith." It doesn't matter what the weights may be. To win in the Kingdom, we must be focused. We have to decide to let the weights go and be willing to allow God to change us into the Kingdom-minded, cultural-changers that we are. The time for excuses has expired. We now understand that our hearts have to be changed and purified by God. A heart knows its own bitterness. We must be willing to change our minds and lives in order to bring change to others' minds and lives. We must have our faith rooted and grounded in the Word of God. Those that we are around daily are the witnesses that will be paying attention to see if our walk aligns with our talk.

On all of the seven mountains of God, there must be found faith-based, compassionate and loving believers who mean business in their walk with God and in the Kingdom. We have to have patience with ourselves as well as others in order to be effective runners in this race. The good news is that we are not alone. We have sisters and brothers that are in the same race – we have spiritual sisters and brothers who share our same spiritual, Holy Spirit-birthed DNA. We are to draw strength from each other with honesty and integrity.
Matured, Kingdom-mindset Christians are capable of proper conduct and accountability for their actions. They understand the call on their lives and give God total pre-eminence. They share the love of God and

MANDATE TO INVADE THE 7 MOUNTAINS OF GOD

show His lovingkindness by shining light in the dark places where deception, greed, and all types of evil are remaining. We are appointed, ordained, and equipped with power from God to succeed in overthrowing these things with great qualifications in victory after victory. We are equipped with wisdom, knowledge, and understanding that establishes the power that works within us. Our walk with our Father is not always an easy one, but it is doable. Practicing obedience is what it takes. We must be doers of the word not just hearers only. We have to keep our hearts pure so that we do not compromise our relationship with our Father. Speak Truth to those on your mountain. God has trusted you to do this.

Each member of the Body of Christ must know the level of authority that they are trained and matured in, so that they may be effective in producing manifestations of Kingdom directives on whatever mountain He has placed them. To take that mountain, he or she should study the Word of the Lord in order to take influential steps in overtaking his/her assigned mountain. With respect to the Word, we all must understand that the word is alive and full of light, and that we must consistently take in and meditate on it. As we do, we become one with that Light.

I would love to see in this end time all believers in Jesus Christ focus on becoming Kingdom-minded. As we do, God Himself will restore Media, Religion, Family, Education, Arts and Entertainment, Government and Business back to the plan He originally initiated in the earth. When we are Kingdom-minded, we will obtain the manifold wisdom of God and we can then work to bring love and peace to our mountains. In the Family Mountain, for instance, mothers and fathers will begin to teach their children and grandchildren about how to conduct themselves at home and in their communities at large. They will learn to reverence God and to have respect for themselves and others. They will learn how to speak, dress and carry themselves appropriately. Some may even have to apologize to their children for past parenting failures.

Now we must turn to God. The Father's Word says in 2 Chronicles 7:14-15, "If my people, which are called by my name, shall humble themselves, and pray, and seek my face, and turn from their wicked ways; then will I hear from heaven, and I will heal their land. Now mine eyes shall be open, and mine ears attend unto the prayer that is made in this place."

Indeed, God is calling ALL to repentance in these last days. If we are to truly seize the mountains, then we must make repentance and obedience integral to our lives. According to Romans 8:19, all of creation is groaning in anticipation of the sons of God really manifesting who and what God has called them to be in the earth. The Kingdom of God is depending on us to climb and to thrive on each of our assigned mountain. Therefore, approach your assignment with all the vigor you can muster and show the precious creation of God their Maker and King. Show them that the Person of Jesus Christ was and is real and alive today. Show them that there is salvation, healing, joy, peace and total victory in life with Him.

Let us pray.

Father God, we ask for Your forgiveness concerning Your Kingdom principles that we have not honored in the earth. Please forgive us, Father, for hearing, but not obeying the Voice of Your Spirit and Your Word. Forgive us for sins known and unknown that we committed against You and Your people, that have caused our lives and our culture to be dysfunctional in so many ways. You said in Your Word, Father, that "The Lord is longsuffering and of great mercy, forgiving iniquity and transgression, and by no means clearing the guilty, visiting the iniquity of the fathers upon the children unto the third and fourth generation"

MANDATE TO INVADE THE 7 MOUNTAINS OF GOD

(Numbers 14:18). So, Father, forgive us for not truly understanding what this meant and for opening our lives, our children's lives, and the very life of our nation, to generation after generation of failure, sin, setbacks and limitations. WE REPENT – we change our minds – and ask you for wisdom, knowledge, understanding and an obedient spirit to correct what is wrong. Give us hearts after Your heart, that we may be restored back to You and each other. And we ask that we might help others find the same restoration. We pray that all cycles of death and destruction would be removed from our assigned mountain, and therefore, our culture. Father, we accept your forgiveness and we move forward trusting that You will continue to help us to break down every evil barrier on these Mountains. In Jesus' Name. Amen.

NOTES

Chapter Seven: The Government Mountain

John Enlow. *The 7 Mountain Prophecy: Unveiling the Coming Elijah Revolution.* Creation House Publishing Company, Lake Mary, FL. 2008.

Made in the USA
Columbia, SC
04 May 2018